THE
PEARL
OF
Dream
STUDY

Cover Design by
bespokebookcovers.com

ISBN: 978-0-9962166-7-8

THE
PEARL
OF
Dream
STUDY

Del Hall and Del Hall IV

Nature Awareness School

Manifest Your Divine Nature

UPLIFT
WITH DREAMS

F.U.N. Inc.

Acknowledgments

It is with the deepest love and gratitude we thank all those who contributed to this book. The willingness to share some of their sacred experiences made this book possible. These testimonies show that so much more is possible in your relationship with God. We hope that reading them will inspire you to more fully accept the Hand of God.

The authors would also like to thank all those who helped in the editing of this book: Joan Clickner, Lorraine Fortier, and Terry Kisner. Your keen eyes and thoughtful suggestions made a huge difference in the telling of these heartwarming stories.

"The days of any religion or path coming between me and my children are coming to an end" saith the Lord

December 29, 2013

Table of Contents

Section Three - Awake Dreams

Section Four - Healing

Section Five - Comfort 107

Section Six - Visiting Loved Ones in Dreams 141

Section Seven - Past-Life and Prophetic Dreams 165

Section Eight - Experiences With the Light of God 195

Summary - The Pearl of Dream Study ...

Foreword

When I was growing up I was taught dreams were just the brain processing the day while I was asleep. I was also taught God does not really "talk" to us anymore. When I was told He stopped that two thousand years ago I was very disappointed. Occasionally in the last two thousand years it seemed God would talk to a saint, but it was implied that saints were some kind of special people and God only talked to them, not us. The spiritual path seemed to be about making sure you followed all the rules, if you could keep them straight, and you did not mess up. Even then you were not sure exactly what that got you. We believed or wondered if God was there, but there was no real communication or love.

That all began to change for me in the early 1990s when two of my friends met Del Hall, who is now God's true Prophet. He had talked to my friends for a long time about God, HU, dreams, true Prophets, different Heavens, and more. When my friends came home they excitedly shared much of what they had learned with me. One thing that really stood out to me then was the idea that dreams are actually real experiences in God's Heavens, or planes, while our bodies are asleep, not just random brain activity. Del had also explained that true Prophets of God can meet with us and work with us in dreams. Something about all that struck a chord in me and I believed it and hoped it could happen to me too.

Soon after that I had a dream in which I met Del and his wife Lynne just after they had finished teaching a spiritual class. At this point I had never met Del or Lynne physically, nor had I ever even seen a picture of them or been to any spiritual class or retreat. In the dream the students were milling around afterwards and I was alone talking with Del and Lynne. Del recommended a book whose title I did not remember when I awoke. Then the dream ended.

I woke up astonished, immediately realizing I had just experienced what my friends had shared. I knew it was real, and I could hardly believe it had happened to me. I had just met Del in a dream! I never looked at dreams the same again. Now that I knew they were real, I started trying to understand what I was being shown in them. I have had thousands of dreams since in which God's Prophet has given me help, guidance, and answers to questions and problems in all areas of my life. I have come to see dreams as an ever-present source of Divine guidance in my life, to make my life better, and to help me learn and grow. They have become a part of the fabric of my life and that of my family. In the most special of these dreams I have felt God's profound Love for me in its purity coming through His Prophet, touching me deeply, and leaving a lasting impression. Through these dreams, with the blessings and insights they contain, God is demonstrating His Love for me. He is taking an active and personal interest in my life and is communicating with me. Wow!

That one original dream was the turning point of my life, and my life since has been completely transformed. From that moment on I became the seeker. I now knew there was something more to life that was real and incredible and I was hungry to find out what it was. Little did I know how amazing it would be. If what Del had told my friends about dreams had been true, then the rest of what he told them must also be true.

I started attending spiritual retreats at the Nature Awareness School a few years later. Under the Prophet's very careful guidance I have been given experiences with the Divine and received help understanding and applying them to my life. Through these experiences I have been given the chance to know for myself that God is real and I am never alone no matter how it seems.

There is a huge difference between knowing and believing - it changes everything. When I was ready Prophet took me home to God in full consciousness via spiritual travel to experience God's Love. Prophet took me again and again until I could fully accept that God truly loved me. One day it finally sank in and I accepted the truth. GOD loves me! On my knees before God the Father, in that profound and loving presence, I knew for sure that I was loved by God no matter what. There was great peace and fulfillment in that love.

GOD loves me and will always love me, no matter what. That is the truth. It is impossible to fully explain God's Love or its impact when it is accepted. It is pure, unconditional, and unchangeable. It will never end or diminish. Nothing will ever replace it or can substitute for it. There is true security and peace beyond all description within God's Love. It gives life, joy, hope, meaning, and purpose. It can change what nothing else seems to be able to change. It transforms, heals, blesses, uplifts, and gives freedom. There is very simply nothing like it.

Prophet has shown me my own Divine nature. I am Soul, an eternal being with a God-given Divine nature. "So God created man in his *own* image." Genesis 1:27 KJV He gave me an experience of myself as that eternal spiritual being God created, and in this experience I knew I go on no matter what. Death is not the end nor are one hundred thousand deaths; whether physical, mental, emotional, or social. That changes a lot. Many fears just dropped away. I can also see that same divinity in everyone else now. You are Soul too.

Prophet has also shown me what was in my heart. He carefully pulled aside the layers of human desires, shortcomings, fears, and insecurities I had picked up over lifetimes. I could then see the great love I have for God and the deep desire I have to be a refined instrument for God so that others may be blessed. That is the fulfillment of my existence. In serving God and being a blessing to others I have found myself, who I really am. What a gift. I have not lost anything, and in fact, I have gained everything. There is great peace in knowing with certainty what is truly in my heart.

The key to all of this has been the Prophet in both his inner and outer form, but mostly his inner form. Even before I knew who or what he was, he was working with me, guiding me, and blessing my path and me. He has been showing me the way home to God and giving me the experiences, including dreams, I needed to grow. He has been protecting me, especially from myself, so I could stay on the path I desire in my heart. He has been teaching me what my experiences mean, about the Divine principles I need to know to live a balanced and abundant life, and about what I could aspire to spiritually. He has also healed me of many of the burdens I was carrying from this lifetime and others. I now walk more freely and with more joy through life, and very importantly, I have been comforted when I truly needed it in the face of my fears, mistakes, and apparent setbacks.

God, through His Prophet, has made real a life I never knew could be possible: To know God my true Father, to know His Love, to hear His Voice daily in my heart and know it, to know His constant Presence through the comforting presence of His Prophet, to have purpose, and to live a life of being an instrument of God's Love and truth to others. I am blessed beyond all comprehension.

With Prophet a life like this is possible for you too. Thank you God for sending your Prophet to find me. Thank you Prophet for taking me home to God. Thank you also to my two friends who helped me get started in this lifetime.

Written by Bobby Clickner

Preface

One of the many ways God demonstrates His Love to us, His children, is by providing guidance, help, and answers to questions and problems in dreams. Few realize that God's Prophet is the one who carries out God's wish and actually provides the dreams. As you read this book the term God's Prophet, or Prophet, or the Prophet will come up often, especially in the actual dreams we share. The following part of this preface will provide you, the reader, with an introductory understanding of God's chosen Prophet. God ALWAYS has a Prophet of His choice on Earth, so whether you are interested in dreams or not, this information may be helpful to your overall spiritual journey.

YOU can truly have an ABUNDANT LIFE through a personal and loving relationship with God, the Holy Spirit, and God's Prophet. This is my primary message to you as the current Prophet. Having a closer relationship with the Divine requires understanding the "Language of the Divine." God expresses His Love in many different and sometimes very subtle ways. The focus of this book is on how He expresses Love through the language of dreams. Often God's Love goes unrecognized and unaccepted because His language is not well known. The dream testimonies in this book will show you some of the ways in which God expresses Love. After reading this book you will know that your relationship with God has the potential to be more profound, more personal, and more loving than any organized religion on Earth currently teaches.

All the dream testimonies in this book were written by my students at the Nature Awareness School. It is here that the nature of God, the Holy Spirit, and the nature of Soul are EXPERIENCED under my guidance as a true Prophet of God. The Nature Awareness School is NOT a religion, it is a school. God and His Prophet are NOT disparaging of any religion of love. However, the more a path defines itself with its teachings, dogma, or tenets, the more walls it inadvertently creates between the seeker and God. Sometimes it even puts God into a smaller box. God does not fit in any box. The Prophet is for all Souls and is purposely not officially aligned with any path but shows respect to all.

An introductory understanding of God's handpicked and divinely trained Prophet is necessary to fully benefit from reading this book. God ALWAYS has a Prophet of His choice on Earth. Each of God's Prophets throughout history has had a unique mission. One may only have a few students with the sole intent to keep God's teachings and truth alive. God may use another to change the course of history. God's Prophets are usually trained by both the current and former Prophets. The Prophet is tested and trained over a very long period of time. The earlier Prophets are physically gone but teach the new Prophet in the inner spiritual worlds. This serves two main purposes: the trainee becomes very adept at spiritual travel and gains wisdom from those in whose shoes he will someday walk. This is vital training because the Prophet is the one who must safely prepare and then take his students into the Heavens and back both in dreams and in guided contemplations.

There are many levels of Heaven, also called planes or mansions. The first Heaven is often referred to as the Astral plane. Even on just that one plane of existence there are over one hundred sub-planes. This Heaven is where most people go after passing unless they receive training while still here in their physical body. Without a guide who is trained properly in the ways of God, a student could misunderstand the intended lesson and become confused as to what is truth. The inner worlds are enormous compared to the physical worlds. They are very real and can be explored safely in dreams when guided by God's Prophet.

Part of my mission is to share more of what is spiritually possible for you as a child of God. Few Souls know or understand that God's Prophet can safely guide God's children, while still alive physically, to their Heavenly Home. Taking a child of God into the Heavens is not the job of clergy. Clergy have a responsibility to pass on the teachings of their religion exactly as they were taught, not to add additional concepts or possibilities. If every clergy member taught their own personal belief system no religion could survive for long. Then the beautiful teachings of an earlier Prophet of God would be lost. Clergy can be creative in finding interesting and uplifting ways to share their teachings, but their job is to keep their religion intact. However, God sends His Prophets to build on the teachings of His past Prophets, to share God's Light and Love, to teach His language, and to guide Souls to their Heavenly Home.

Some of my students share experiences in this book of when they were taken to God's Temples of learning in their dreams. It is here, in these higher worlds, where they experience God's truths at a depth of knowingness beyond what is possible by studying physical scripture alone. After reaching this level of spiritual experience, physical scripture comes alive with truth at new and higher levels. At this point one actually values scripture more than they could have possibly valued it before having their own personal experience.

There is ALWAYS MORE when it comes to God's teachings and truth. No one Prophet can teach ALL of God's ways. It may be that the audience of a particular time in history cannot absorb more wisdom. It could be due to a Prophet's limited time to teach and limited time in a physical body on Earth. Ultimately, it is that there is ALWAYS MORE! Each of God's Prophets bring additional teachings, opportunities, and ways to draw closer to God, building on the work and teachings of former Prophets. That is one reason why Prophets of the past ask God to send another to comfort, teach, and continue to help God's children grow into greater abundance. Former Prophets continue to have great love for God's children and want to see them continue to grow in accepting more of God's Love. One never needs to stop loving or accepting help from a past Prophet in order to grow with the help of the current Prophet. All true Prophets of God work together and help one another to do God's work.

Prophet Del Hall III

Introduction

"Parable of the Apple"

Deep down you know "there is more"

When I was growing up the choices for apples were simple: Red Delicious or Golden Delicious. But I came to the conclusion very early on there was nothing delicious about them, especially the Red Delicious. It was not until years later I came to learn they were not grown for flavor but for their ability to be picked early, shipped across country, and still look pretty on the shelf. Flavor was not the highest consideration.

Even though my experience with apples available on the supermarket shelf did not reflect it, somewhere deep inside I knew it was a good fruit. I had faith there was more to the apple; how could there not be? For the most part they served their purpose, but they still felt hollow to me, a shell of their true glorious potential. Looking back, I do not even remember if I believed there was a good apple out there somewhere, but I knew what I currently had was lacking something.

Life can be like this for many. On the surface it is good or perhaps even great. They have a good job, a loving family, hobbies, friends, a nice house, enjoyable vacations, fellowship at church, a belief in God, and there can be genuine joy in all of it. But still, something nibbles at them. It is the feeling that there is more. What is it they are missing? It is not a negative reflection on our current lives to consider there could be more. There is always more! Our life can be even more abundant.

Somewhere along the way the stores started carrying Granny Smiths, Gala, and Fuji. I am sure I recognized this as an improvement to the state of the apple, yet it still did not fill the void. Something was still lacking. The apple had still not manifested its true potential for me.

Years later I was driving down a country road in Virginia and came across an orchard and packing shed that specialized in heirloom Virginia apples. I'm not even sure how I ended up there, but I still remember it vividly. I walked up to a table with cases of apple varieties I had never heard of before. The owner came out and I began excitedly picking his brain with all sorts of questions. It turns out they had over two hundred varieties of apples that you cannot get at your local store. This in itself blew my mind as

I could probably only list a dozen varieties I had previously heard of. Many of the apples on the table before me were grown in the orchards of our founding fathers, which touched me on many levels.

The owner took out his pocketknife and sliced off pieces of one after another after another for me to try. As he handed them to me I could feel his joy in being able to share them; he knew what it was he was offering. I sampled dozens of phenomenal apples that afternoon with a variety and depth of flavor that was absolutely incredible. When I eventually left for home my heart was as full of gratitude and contentment as the car was loaded with paper bags full of treasure.

When I was sampling apples that day it literally almost brought me to tears. In retrospect it wasn't so much the flavors that moved me. It was the "knowing" I had been carrying all these years that there was more to the apple. My "knowing" had been shown to be true. At this point in my life I had probably even forgotten this knowing I carried, but when I tasted these flavors it all came back. There was more! My heart knew it and here it was, right in front of me. I had faith the apple was indeed a good fruit.

After all these years here was the proof, and how sweet it was!

I share this story because this book could be like my trip to the orchard for some of you. There is more to dreams and to life in general; deep down you know there is. You are more than just your physical body; you are an eternal spiritual being created out of the Light and Love of God.

The truths contained in the stories within this book can pull back the curtain and prove your heart right. God loves you and you are not alone, nor are you forgotten. God always has someone here on Earth to help show you the way home to Him.

Del Hall IV

Fundamentals of Dream Study

Cultures for thousands of years have looked to their dreams for guidance, healing, personal insight, and wisdom from God. In this section we cover: The long and rich history of dreams, how Soul can travel the Heavens in dreams, how to prepare yourself before falling asleep, the benefit of a personal dream journal, and dream interpretation.

1

Dream Study is Not New

Society displays short-term memory when it considers dream study only a new-age trend. Dream study is actually quite the opposite. Cultures for thousands of years have looked to their dreams for guidance, healing, personal insight, and wisdom from God. They knew dreams were a window into Heaven and that their daily lives and relationships with God could be improved by looking to the wisdom in their dreams.

Some of the oldest recorded information on dream study is from the Sumerians in ancient Mesopotamia. The clay tablets they used to record information on dreams are over five thousand years old, dating back to 3100 BC. Mesopotamians believed that Soul left the body while sleeping to travel into the spiritual worlds. They indeed were right.

Ancient Egyptians wrote down their dreams on papyrus as far back as 2000 BC. The "Egyptian Book of Dreams" is one of the oldest recorded documents in existence, dating back to the early reign of Ramses II (1279-1213 BC). People during this time who had vivid dreams were considered blessed. Ancient Egyptians practiced "dream incubation," which simply meant they slept on special "dream beds" at a temple in hopes of receiving a dream. They would then meet with a special priest, known as a "Master of Secret Things" who was a dream interpreter, to seek wisdom from the dream. The fact that they made the effort to travel to a holy temple to be "closer to God," in hopes of receiving a dream, illustrates how they considered dreams to be of Divine origin.

In the Bible in the Gospel of Saint Matthew, an angel of the Lord visits Joseph on multiple occasions to bless him with guidance and support. First by letting Joseph know that Mary was with child. Then by instructing him to take Mary to Egypt and then, when it was safe, to return to Israel. People quote "the angel of the Lord appeared unto Joseph" all the time, but more often than not they leave off the next three words, "in a dream." The story of God guiding Joseph and Mary through a dream is but one of over one hundred references to dreams and visions in the Bible. A close study of them reveals the Lord spoke to people of all societal levels, not just Pharaoh or Prophets. The same is true today; God can communicate with each and every one of us personally through a dream, or a "vision of the night."

There are many people who believe the Lord can communicate through dreams, but sadly they do not feel it could happen to them. They feel that yes indeed God can speak with Joseph to keep Jesus safe, or to one of His Prophets, but to believe that God would reach out to them is just too much – practically blasphemy. I can assure you it is not. This in no way is a slight to God's Prophets; rather it is a testament to God's Love for all Souls. God is a living God who loves each and every one of us. He continues to reach out and offer us His Love, guidance, support, healing, protection, and insight. For many this is too much to accept at first, but with time you can come to know this truth for yourself.

It is not the focus of this book to paint the full picture of the history of dream study. For those who are interested there are countless books entirely on the subject and it is a fascinating story. Almost every religion and culture throughout all of recorded history has references to dreams. This demonstrates that the idea of God communicating through dreams is not a new concept. It is only within the last half-century or so that dreams have been thought of more and more as residual mind-junk from your day, or the expression of repressed desires or unconscious wish fulfillment. While you can certainly learn about your heart's desires in dreams, to look at dreams as purely mind-generated would be forfeiting the opportunity for Divine guidance and a closer relationship with God.

Regardless of what the world in general may think, dreams are of great value to those seeking more from life. The tools, truths, and examples in this book will help you to utilize this eternal source of wisdom for yourself.

2

You are Soul

Saint Paul said he knew a man who was drawn up to the third Heaven. Actually it was Saint Paul himself - he did not want to brag. If there is a third heaven, how about a first, second, third, fourth, fifth, and so on. Jesus said, "In my Father's house are many mansions." John 14:2 KJV Whether you call them mansions, Heavens, planes, realms, spheres, or inner worlds etc., it is not as cut and dried as simply "Heaven" and "Earth." The worlds of God are vast and you can learn to safely explore them in dreams with Prophet.

A key to understanding, or at least for now considering, how dreams are actually experiences within the greater worlds of God, not just residual "mid-junk" from your day is the following truth: *You do not have a Soul; you are Soul.* You have a car, you have a house, you have a job, but you do not have a Soul, you are Soul. To say you "have" a Soul is to subjugate the divinity of Soul to the human earthy vessel. You are Soul first. When this body wears out,

Soul will carry on, It is eternal. Soul is the individual manifested being-ness of the Holy Spirit. You are Soul, an eternal Divine spark that God placed temporarily into a human body. You are not God, nor will you ever become God, but in a very real sense you, as Soul, are a piece of the Voice of God, or the Holy Spirit. Soul is twenty-four seven; it does not sleep. Soul can leave Its earthly vessel and travel into the Heavens while the body rests.

Some have a hard time accepting the truth of their true spirituality because of their shortcomings or the mistakes they have made here in the physical world. They lose sight of their divinity and think, "If I'm so great (as Soul) what then is my problem? If I was truly a spiritual being, I wouldn't have all these challenges." Well, there is spiritual "gravity" down here. Soul gets blinded by the temporal earthly form and trapped by the passions of the mind: fear, greed, guilt, lust, worry, vanity, anger, and excessive attachment. These things can be overpowering which makes them easy to relate to, but these negative passions are not the real you. They are the mind-junk. You are not your imperfections. You are not your defilements. You are Soul, a Divine child of God. As Soul you can travel the Heavens with Prophet in dreams.

3

Before Falling Asleep

Dreams are one of the ways God communicates information to us, His children. Therefore it is worth asking for a dream before falling asleep. Most people do dream, even if they do not recall having dreams. By asking for a dream before sleep you are inviting the Divine more fully into your life and the chance of remembering the dream increases. Asking for Divine guidance every night is a way to draw closer to God, and God does respond!

You can ask for a dream that is in your best spiritual interest and leave it at that. You can also ask for something specific. Perhaps there is something you need help with, such as a relationship, a job, health concern, or some other decision in life. One may also ask for higher understanding of a spiritual truth or to be shown God's ways and truths in general. It is a good idea to also ask, "Please help me remember my dream tonight." Gaining clarity is such a blessing, and one way God's Prophet can deliver it to us is through dreams.

Doing your part to become more receptive to remembering and understanding your dreams is also very important. One of the best ways to become more receptive and spiritualize yourself before bed is to sing HU. HU is an ancient name for God that can be sung quietly or aloud in prayer. HU has existed since the beginning of time in one form or another and is available to all regardless of religion. It is a pure way to express your love to God and give thanks for your blessings. Singing HU (HUUUUUU pronounced hue) serves as a tuning fork with Spirit that brings you into greater harmony with the Divine. Singing HU will raise you up and open you up spiritually, which makes you more receptive to the guidance and Love of God, and to God's Prophet. All the authors in this book sing HU daily in spiritual contemplation.

Singing HU for a few minutes also nourishes Soul, your true eternal self. Reading of scripture or simply thinking of something you are grateful for before bed will also make you more receptive to receiving and remembering a dream. God speaks to our hearts, and an open heart can "hear" better. Gratitude is a great way to open your heart and fortunately there is always something to be grateful for.

4

Your Dream Journal

Anyone serious about cultivating a richer dream life needs a dream journal. It is a must-have, like a hammer is for a carpenter. Without it not much will get done. It does not have to have a purple unicorn on it, although it most certainly can if that is your thing. It can really be most anything from a nice leather journal to a spiral bound notebook. Whatever you go with treat it with respect. Yes, it is just paper and ink, but more than that it is a collection of your sacred experiences and insights from God.

Your journal should live beside your bed within arms reach. When you awake from a dream it can be hard enough to disturb the warmth of sleep and take a few moments to record it, even harder if it requires getting out of bed and finding your journal. Put it next to the bed, opened to the next blank page with your pen or pencil. It is also nice to have a flashlight handy. Rather than turn on a bright overhead light and disturb others, or yourself, a flashlight is a great way to go.

Anything worthwhile in life takes discipline to develop. If you want to be physically healthier it requires making conscious choices in regards to diet and exercise. If your heart is set on a certain occupation it goes without saying you need certain training or degrees. If you desire to play a certain instrument it requires practice. Those who love sports know sitting on the couch all day is not going to improve their game. It is no different with dream study. If you are interested or at least curious enough about dreams to give it a try, then make the effort. Get a journal, put it by the bed, wake from your sleep, and write your dreams down. On a related note, some find a tape recorder works better for them.

Often the dream will be forgotten as soon as the conscious mind awakes and starts thinking about getting up, getting dressed, and about the day ahead. So it is best to record your dream before getting up and going for the day. Write whatever you have, even if the meaning is not known or does not even make sense. In other words, write it down now - make sense of it later. That being said, there are times when it is best to awaken from a dream and just lie there, still in that moment of clarity, before the conscious mind awakes. Gently reflect on the dream and sometimes you will arrive at its meaning.

Sometimes the specifics of the dream are forgotten, but the overall message is received and understood. Be sure to also note any feelings that accompanied the dream. Did you feel relieved, nervous, exited, etc.? Was there a strong smell, sound, or color that stood out? Did a particular person, song, country, time of year, etc. stand out? All of this information may help you to understand the message behind the dream.

That being said, you must also learn to follow your heart on when enough is enough. To lie there for two or three hours every morning recording every detail of a dream is unrealistic and out of balance. All life is about learning how to "Walk in Balance and Harmony," and this applies to journaling as well. There are times when a very small detail of a dream is very important to note, and other times when the big picture will do just fine. An example of this would be recording "I was driving a blue four wheel drive Chevy pickup in the dream." Perhaps even noting the year, model, and the engine size versus "I was driving a truck." Again, learning how to follow your heart in this matter is key. Sometimes details matter and sometimes they do not.

One of the biggest blocks that keep people

from writing down their dream is they only remember a small fragment of it. They figure why sit up, turn the light on, and write down something as seemingly insignificant as "I had a dream where I was cutting firewood." More often than not if you actually sit up and make the effort to write down the one small piece you have, more will come. As soon as you write down "I was cutting firewood" the memories often flood back in, and before you know it you are scribbling away with your pen trying to keep up with the remembrance. A seemingly short snippet of a memory turns into "I was cutting firewood when my friend Anthony showed up. He told me about a big oak tree that had fallen across the street. We loaded up our gear and went to clear the road so folks could get through. When we were cutting up the tree a huge black bear comes out of the woods and just stops and stares at us. It was then, in the dream, I remembered an experience I had as a child where I saw a bear chasing our sheep through the back field…" and on and on.

God is not just going to hand out truth and wisdom to those who are not interested. Making the effort to show Spirit you care enough to write down what you do remember shows God you indeed care. Your efforts will be more than matched.

It is also good to note that your biggest enemy is your mind and its ruts. The mind does not like change. Often truth contained within dreams can lead to change, and the mind would rather not have any of that. You will need to learn to work around the mind. Writing down one small fragment of a dream is a perfect example of this, even though your mind is saying, "Don't waste your time writing this one down, you don't remember enough of it." You are not your mind, you are Soul. Mind is a useful servant but a terrible master.

There are times when during the course of a day, a dream will come flooding back into your consciousness. When this happens see it as another opportunity to reflect on its meaning. Also take a moment to consider what you are doing or thinking about at the exact moment the memory returns. Sometimes there is a correlation. What you are doing at the time might help to better understand the dream's meaning and to what part of your life it relates.

There is a very practical element to a dream journal. It affords you the opportunity to go back and review your dream history. When you have six weeks, six months, two years, ten years, or more worth of dreams you have the opportunity to go back and look for the big picture. Sometimes a dream that made no sense by itself might later deliver its message when reviewed in context and combined with other dreams or life experiences. Sometimes we are not ready to accept the truth in a dream or even have a reference point for its meaning. By having a dream journal to review we may be able to go back and understand earlier dreams. A dream journal can become a treasured possession. When we look back through it and see all the times Spirit reached out to us to comfort and guide us, it serves as a reminder that God loves us and we are not alone. Whether recorded or not, our most precious experiences with the Divine should be etched in our hearts. Our remembrance of them will continue to nourish us more than just ink on a page.

One of the most valuable elements to a dream journal is that it is a form of drawing nigh. The Bible says, "Draw nigh to God, and he will draw nigh to you." James 4:8 KJV. This is a spiritual principle and it is absolutely true. When we reach out to God, God responds. When we do what we can, even though it is small in comparison, God will respond by doing what He can do. A dream journal is very much a form of drawing nigh, and God does respond.

5

Interpretation in General

Dreams are part of God's "Language of the Divine" and it takes time, practice, and effort to gain fluency just like learning any foreign language. Dream interpretation is an art and its language is mostly personal. We are unique individuals with different relationships with God, different reference points, backgrounds, and states of consciousness. Because God loves us He meets us where we are at and communicates in a way He hopes we will understand. With this in mind dream symbol books offer little personal information, although they may be fun to look at. There is not one dream symbol to fit all dreamers.

For example, water usually represents Spirit. Depending on what form it takes: a river, a manmade pool, droplet, rainstorm, whether it is dirty or clean, frozen as snow, etc., tells volumes. However, for someone who almost drowned as a child, water also might represent fear. For someone having health issues, water might be a reminder to drink more. There is no one size fits all with dream symbology. That being said there can be overlap in what dream imagery represents.

Dream study may start with symbols that represent meanings but will eventually transcend symbols to actual experiences. One does not need symbols to understand actual experiences. Try to consider the big picture of your dreams versus such and such means this, and such and such means that. Dreams are way beyond symbols. What you are doing is working towards a clearer communication with the Divine in both the waking and sleeping state. Understanding dreams is about learning to listen better to what Spirit is expressing. Even if a dream is not understood, recognize the gift of love being demonstrated, whether it comes in the form of guidance, insight, comfort, healing, etc. Receiving God's Love is even more important than understanding the information within a dream.

Dreams loosely fall into one of three categories, so when you are trying to interpret a dream consider which of the three feels most likely. Is it about your "daily life," involving everyday events such as your health, job, family, work, etc.? Is it a dream about your negative "passions of the mind" such as: anger, fear, lust, vanity, worry, greed, and excessive attachments? Or is it a "spiritual" dream, one that sheds light on your relationship with God or perhaps involves meeting the Prophet or another spiritual teacher in a dream? Dreams often have at least three meanings. There will be the primary lesson, a secondary, and tertiary meaning.

Dreams can also provide information, healings, and insights in earlier or future timelines. You may be given a dream of an experience from years ago or even your childhood. Perhaps these insights will be helpful in your current life by bringing understanding or peace. Even past life memories can be given in a dream to help you better understand your current life. Your dreams can also be prophetic. These types of dreams may show how current decisions will affect your future.

Dreams may have nothing to do with your daily life; rather they are simply a memory of your inner travels as Soul. Sometimes you may awaken from spiritual traveling and just have no reference or way to understand it mentally. The mind is like a small bucket in comparison to the vast ocean of the inner dream worlds and cannot hold it all when waking. One of the best examples to describe this is of a man living in a two-dimensional world having a dream of a sphere. How would he be able to describe this or understand it upon awakening? Soul would know, but the mind would not have a reference for it. You can however ask for help understanding your dreams. Sing HU and ask God's Prophet for clarity - often this will help.

The biggest block to understanding dreams is our mind. While Soul craves truth and growth, the mind is fearful of change and of very direct truth about itself. The mind would rather keep things as they are and not rock the boat. It sometimes acts as a censor and tries to shield you from what it thinks would be too much truth. One of the ways Spirit gets around the mind is by having the characters in our dreams actually be ourselves in disguise. It is easier to accept a truth about ourselves in this way. When trying to understand a dream with other people involved, assume they represent you as a starting point. Perhaps their actions are actually the way you act in similar situations.

If your dreams are unclear or mostly symbolic at this point, worry not. They can move to a place of clarity where little interpretation is needed. The more you spiritualize yourself by singing HU or developing an attitude of gratitude, the clearer they will become. This is a sign of your inner spiritual worlds coming into order and a shift from operating primarily from the mind to Soul. Dreams are often a reflection of your waking state. As you spiritualize your actions and thoughts in waking life it spills over into the dream worlds. In time you will see the continuity between the two. However, no matter how far one goes in dream study you will still sometimes have confusing dreams.

Soul knows truth and it has a "truth detector" of sorts. It is that small voice inside of everyone. When followed, some call it "following ones heart." As you nourish Soul by singing HU you begin to trust your truth detector more and more. Eventually the real you, Soul, will guide your understanding of dreams more than the mind. So we now have both the mind and Soul, often referred to as our heart, to help us understand dream guidance. Let us now add one more component to dream interpretation: emotions. When interpreting a dream consider how you felt upon awakening. Were you scared, relieved, nervous, joyful, etc.?

Keep in mind not every dream contains something of value worth pursuing. At the end of the day a dream may also be "just a dream." It might simply be a test to see if you buy into a seed of doubt or will waste your time. If you do feel the dream is important, you have contemplated on it and still do not get a meaning, ask Prophet to please communicate this message again in another dream.

The absolute best way to gain fluency and understanding of your dreams is to keep at it. With every dream you write down and with every dream you make the effort to understand, you are going to get better at interpretation. The beauty of this book is that it contains over fifty examples of actual dreams and their meanings. Even though they are not your own dreams they will still help paint a picture of how Spirit works in dreams. Each one will broaden your reference system.

To help the reader understand the value of dreams this book has been organized into seven different sections of dreams: Guidance and personal insights, awake dreams, healing dreams, comforting dreams, dreams with loved ones who have passed, past-life and prophetic dreams, and dreams of experiencing the Light of God. Reading them with an open heart and mind can help you better understand your own dreams, as well as open you to grander possibilities of what dreams can do for you.

Guidance and Personal Insights

Dreams can provide a window of opportunity for God to guide you through the challenges of daily life. There is no area or challenge too small or insignificant to receive guidance or clarity on. If it is important to you, it is important to God. Whether it is help with a career, a relationship, a health concern, or any of the other countless things that come up in life. Guidance through dreams can also come in the form of warning and protection. Ultimately though, dreams can guide you to know your true eternal self, Soul, by removing blocks to your continued growth and happiness and show you the way home to God.

You are so much more than your physical body. You are Soul, an eternal child of God who has come into this world to grow in your ability to give and receive love. However, the "spiritual gravity" down here is heavy and it is quite common to become blinded to your divinity and your potential as a point of light. In fact, almost everything in this physical world is designed to distract you from manifesting your true spiritual potential. Many fall into operating more from the mind with all its ruts rather than from the heart as Soul. It is hard for Soul to soar free like an eagle when it has become buried under the passions of the mind: fear, worry, vanity, anger, lust, and excessive attachment, to name a few.

One of the greatest benefits of dream study is receiving help overcoming the things holding us back spiritually. Often we are not even aware of the things holding us back from a more abundant life. In dreams the Prophet can show us where we stand spiritually, if we are receptive. We can also be shown opportunities for growth, learn from our mistakes, and be reminded of our true spiritual goals and our highest spiritual potential. What an amazing opportunity dreams are: personalized gifts of love from God in the form of guidance and insights to help make life run smoother and lead us toward true happiness, abundance, and purpose.

By doing your part to stay spiritually nourished and by making the effort to remember, record, and review them you can more fully benefit from the blessings of dreams.

6

God's Plan "Flies" Best

*This story is a great testimony to the personal element
of dreams. God can reach out to us through dreams
and bless us with understanding and insight. All areas
of our lives can be improved. Dreams are timely gifts of
love tailor-made for us.*

This dream was given to me one night during
a spiritual retreat I attended. At that time I was in
transition between careers. I was preparing to
retire from one job and making plans to start a
part-time business. In the dream I saw a small
airplane upside down on the ground. The pilot
crawled out from underneath. He survived the
crash but I noticed the front wing was very small.
It was no wider than the body of the airplane. He
said it was his own experimental design. Well, it
obviously did not work.

I prayed for God's help understanding the
dream and shared it in class at the retreat. I was
shown that the pilot was myself. I was relying on
my own intellect alone, rather than God's

strength. Later I realized that one of the ways I was doing this was in designing the plans for my career change myself and hoping that it would just take off. This dream was a Divine gift received just in time. It showed me the results of what could happen in my life if I continued the way I was going. I was relying solely on my own efforts without inviting God's help, specifically in this major life change. That is like trying to fly with a tiny wing of my own design.

I prayed for Divine help in the career transition and surrendered my own plans. That is when things began to fall into place. I could see the Hand of God smoothing the way and doors began to open. I have become aware that the Hand of God, in the form of the inner Prophet, is always with me. As I responded and did my part the original plans changed into something a lot more enjoyable and stable. It manifested into a new job with excellent benefits and the freedom to do more of the things I wanted to do.

I am so grateful for this dream and to know God loves me and wants to help me avoid the pitfalls of life. Knowing that inspires me to rely more fully on Prophet in all areas of my life and to help him share God's Love with others.

Written by Paul Harvey Sandman

7

Dream Warning Provides Protection

There are times when one can be given advance warning in a dream. God can reach out and protect us by making us aware of upcoming danger. The following is a classic example.

In this dream I was driving to work on a familiar piece of highway. A large tractor-trailer came speeding up on my right and began coming into my lane. He apparently did not see me. The truck kept coming over and nearly pushed me into the guardrails on my left. I slowed abruptly to avoid a collision and began to move over into the right lane. At this point another car came up on my left and made a quick cut in front of me to get off the exit ramp.

In a short period of time I had two close calls where I had to react quickly to avoid an accident. I woke up and was still a bit shaken with a vivid recollection of this dream. On my way to work that morning, in an area very similar to the dream, I saw a tractor-trailer coming up on my right. I remembered the dream so I slowed down well before he got alongside of me. He then swerved into the lane I had just been in. I was watching for a second car at this point and saw it come up on the left and make the abrupt crossover to exit the freeway. Both of these things happened just like in the dream. The only difference was that I was safely behind the truck and the second car, thanks to the warning in the dream.

I was very blessed and my day was so different because I was an observer of this situation from a safe distance. It was all due to the heads-up I received in the dream. I was protected from a potentially tragic crash because I paid attention to this communication from God, took it seriously, and remembered it later in the day. Our dreams are real. If we dismiss or brush aside the information they contain we could be missing a valuable gift. A gift that could change our life or maybe even save it.

Written by Lorraine Fortier

8

Help Finding a New Home

For those who understand and pay attention to the "Language of the Divine," life can be a joy to live. Whether through a nighttime dream or an awake dream, this loving guidance is available at every step on the journey through life. It provides the insight we need for a smooth passage and serves as a constant reminder - we are loved and we are not alone.

A couple years ago my fiancé and I decided to relocate from Massachusetts to Virginia. After identifying the general area we felt would be a good place to live and build a business, we began our search for a house to rent.

Two months prior to our anticipated move we flew to Virginia with a list of houses we hoped to see in our short visit to the area. On our way to the first house on our list, a "for rent" sign in front of another house caught my eye. The front door was wide open so we stopped. The owners happened to be packing their car with a few last things before moving to Massachusetts, of all places. We were met with a warm welcome and gracious offer to be shown around. It turned out the house was not right for us, but the experience stood out as an awake dream, a communication from the Divine, reminding us to stay flexible and alert to other "open doors" of opportunity that may catch our attention along the way.

This sense of adventure stayed with us as the day unfolded. Everything just flowed. Planned stops interwoven with unexpected detours and surprises as if we were being led from one open door to the next. Toward the end of the day I followed an inner nudge to explore a neighborhood on the other side of town where, as far as we knew, there were no available houses for rent. To our surprise we came upon a "for rent" sign in front of a gray house with an unusual roofline. When we pulled up, the license plate "OPNLOCK" on the vehicle in front of us caught my attention. The front door was wide open and workmen were coming and going. One of them directed us to the landlord who happened to be working on-site that day. Although the house had just been rented, when he heard what we were looking for, he suggested another house he had nearby which was not quite ready yet. As it turned out it was the perfect house for us, in the perfect location, at the perfect price.

Later that night as I leafed through my dream journal before bed I came across a sketch I'd scribbled upon waking from a dream a few days prior. It depicted a gray house with an unusual roofline located where two main routes intersected, an exact description of the house where we met our future landlord that day. To me this was an added layer of reassurance that we were moving in the right direction, in harmony with God's plan, as we embarked on this major life change.

At the end of the day, any worry I had been carrying about our upcoming move was replaced with trust and a sense of adventure for what lay ahead. Along with this, a gentle knowing that our efforts, coupled with an openness to being led by the Divine along the way, would result in everything working out for the best. Which it has, in every way.

The golden thread of God's Love weaves an abundant life for each of us. Developing our own personal relationship with the Divine is the key that opens the door to a truly blessed life.

Written by Sandra Lane

9

A Career, a Dog, a Husband

Dreams are a source of guidance from the Divine. The wisdom gained by paying attention to them can bless every aspect of your life, everything from relationships to health concerns, finances, careers, family life, and more. In a sense, each and every one of us has our own personal window to Heaven through dreams. Each of the three dreams you are about to read are great examples of this.

Dreams have played a part in my life for many years. Being raised in the family I was blessed to be raised in, I learned to pay attention to my dreams for wisdom and guidance from the Divine. I was at a point in my life where I was trying to decide between career paths. I had been heading toward a career in forensic science and had interviewed at the state laboratory in the city. This was the career I had been working towards for many years. Around the time I was interviewing for this "dream job," I started to get the feeling I may want to do something different. I was now considering staying in academics and applying for a position at a college and pursuing a career in cancer research. I had a dream which reassured me as I made this choice. In the dream, I was in a city and everyone was attacking me - they were driving big trucks and chasing me all around. I was driving a truck and was trying to get away from them. I ended up driving the truck off a cliff and as the truck left the ground I found out I could fly my truck away from the people chasing me. So I steered myself down to safety and landed at a calm and peaceful college campus. When I awoke, I felt calm and peaceful about the new career direction I had been thinking about. I interpreted leaving the chaos of the city and ending up on the college campus as affirmation I was on the right track. I did not make the decision based on this one dream, but the dream gave me the reassurance and peace about considering the other position. Ultimately I chose the career in academics and could not be happier with the choice. I feel it is where I am supposed to be.

Now, about my dog. I was at the point that all pet owners dread. It was time to decide if I should put my dog down. I had an awake dream and a night dream that helped reassure me about this tough decision. My dog Annie was sick and I was going back and forth with the decision. I had been doing this for some time now and really needed to make the choice. I was on my way home one day driving over the mountain and was saying out loud, "Just give me a sign, please God, give me a sign, what should I do?" I really wanted a sign as to the right choice. Right then I looked up and saw a very dark cloud in a bright beautiful blue sky and it was in the shape of a dog laying upside down, looking like it was no longer with us. I thought to myself, "Well then, I guess I did beg for a sign." I was not overly thrilled with the one I got but recognized I had been heard. Then I looked into the sky to the right of that cloud and I saw a bright beautiful shiny cloud that looked like a dog leaping through the sky. I saw this as saying if I make the choice to put her down she will be free and happy.

Around the same time, I also had a dream where my dog was running full speed down a back alley and I called her to come in. She skidded to a stop and came into the fenced yard. She would have preferred to continue her running but did as I asked. I saw this as meaning I was keeping her fenced in and stopping her from being free. It was a hard decision but these dreams helped me accept it was the right thing to do. They gave me comfort that she would be okay.

I had numerous dreams that led me to my husband. I had been praying to find love; I had been single for quite some time and was hoping to have love in my life. Every time I would pray at night about finding love, I would have a dream about a bear. I would wake up and think, "Well that's weird. Am I supposed to marry a bear?" I just filed these away in the back of my head. I did not understand why every time I asked about finding love I had these bear dreams. Then I met Anthony, my now husband. We were on our first date and he "happened" to mention that people usually call him Bear, they have since he was little. Well I very quickly perked up a little bit, and all the memories of these bear dreams came flooding back to me. These dreams alerted me to pay attention and give the date a chance! I realized that I was being shown where I could find love if I chose to. At the time I had the dreams they did not make sense, but by writing them down and remembering them it was now beginning to make sense. We have now been happily married for almost five years.

Written by Emily Allred

10

Door is Opened to Freedom

In a very real sense many people on Earth live in a prison. A prison of consciousness. It is here we are blinded to the divinity within us. It is here we are trapped by the illusion that there is nothing more. It is here we get so wrapped up with the non-stop distractions that even if the prison door were open some would not know to step through it. Fortunately, some do.

I was in my thirties and was experiencing an inner unrest. I did not know or understand at the time what it was but there was something deep within me stirring. I did not know what this unrest was, or how to resolve it. I was seeking something, but what? I had a beautiful family, friends, home, and wonderful comforts but something was calling to me. One night the desperate feeling was so intense I called out in a prayer, "I want to go home." It surprised me, I did not know what this meant, but it came from a place deep within me.

I received a brochure for the Nature Awareness School in the mail a short time after that experience. After some consideration I decided to go and it changed my life in so many good ways. I am blessed with a spiritual teacher who has given me spiritual tools and over time changed the unrest to peace within me. One of the tools given was the study of dreams.

I had a dream that seemed simple but defined me and my journey in life prior to going to the school. In this dream I was in a clean, tidy, comfortable, and nicely decorated room. I looked around and it became apparent that the room was a prison cell. The cell door was open and on the other side was my spiritual teacher, the Prophet, and two other teachers. I was being given the opportunity to get out of the prison cell.

At the time I did not recognize I was living my life as if in a prison cell. My life from all outward appearance was good, yet something inside me knew differently. The prison cell represented things that limited my freedom: fears, worries, vanity, attachments, negative attitudes, as well as unhealed experiences from past lives. I did not realize I was living in a prison cell because it was comfortable and familiar.

In the dream I hesitated to leave the confinement of the cell. I seemed to be frozen in my old familiar ways. When the door started to close I made the decision to leave the confines of the cell and took hold of my spiritual teacher. Through the years he has been teaching me and giving me spiritual tools to use to break free of the prison of human consciousness. Prophet opened a doorway to a new way of living where I now experience love, joy, peace, and a freedom I have never known.

Written by Renée Walker

11

My Priorities Bring Peace

We must make time to connect with God every day to stay nourished. It matters not how busy life gets. If we do not, things fall apart. The following is an excellent testimony on the need for daily spiritual bread.

Whenever I get started on a new project I jump into it wholeheartedly. I develop a type of tunnel vision and focus only on the task ahead. This can be a good attribute in some ways. It allows me to get a lot done in a short amount of time, but is also a detriment in other ways. I become so focused on the task at hand I lose sight of the big picture. Some time back we started a new project at work. We had a really tight deadline and a lot to accomplish. As is my habit, I started pouring more and more energy into the project, sometimes working up to twenty hours a day trying to catch up and get ahead of the problems that kept cropping up. It seemed the harder I tried, the farther behind we were. This pace kept up for several weeks, and I was becoming pretty exhausted.

A very important part of my spiritual practices is spending quality time with Divine Spirit. I set aside time each day to tune in, communicate, and develop a stronger, richer, and deeper relationship with God and God's Voice, the Holy Spirit. This time is essential to keep me in balance, keep my priorities in focus, and reconnect in a meaningful way with the Source of all existence.

As I started working more and more hours, and trying harder and harder to pull this project together, I spent less and less time on my spiritual pursuits. I prayed every day and recognized the presence of the Divine in many of the events of the day, but I was not spending that quality time with Divine Spirit necessary for me to grow stronger in my relationship. I cannot sit idle for long. Very soon the relationship grows weaker as I focus on temporal things and not on Spiritual things.

One night I had a very strong and clear dream. In that dream I felt the presence of Prophet next to me. We were going to look at a house I was planning to move into. The house was very run down. You could not get into the front door as it was in disrepair. Entering the house through the back, the inside was just as bad as the outside; sheetrock was pulled down, the wiring was poor. All in all, it was in bad shape.

When I awoke I contemplated on the meaning of the dream. The dream spoke of the condition of my spiritual life. If I did not make some changes, my spiritual home (life) was going to look like that old, broken down house. The house was not suitable for truly living. Truly living for me is spoken of in the Bible as a "more abundant life." It is a life rich and full, strong in the relationship with the Holy Spirit. Seeking first that relationship is what allows one to truly experience all the blessings God wants to share with us. Focusing on worldly impermanent things, as I was doing and was demonstrated in the dream, produces the opposite.

That day I set aside time for God. I found a quiet place and sang HU, a love song to God. HU is a pure expression of your love to God and a way to give thanks for your blessings. It is not asking for anything, it is not seeking anything from God. It tunes you into Spirit and brings greater harmony with the Divine. I sang HU for a while and then suddenly I received a great gift from God. All the weight and tension I did not even know I was carrying fell off my shoulders. I felt a warm inrush of love, joy, and peace. I saw with clarity what I had been missing. The love and joy that was downloaded to me was an incredible blessing and healing. I accepted those blessings from the Divine with gratitude. I expressed my gratitude for the blessings, my gratitude for the insight and clarity, and my gratitude for the dream that brought me back to my true priorities.

Written by Paul Nelson

12

Breadcrumbs From God

*Sometimes even a seemingly simple dream contains
great wisdom. Through practice we can learn to glean
the pearls of wisdom out of our dreams. Even better,
we have the opportunity for the one who taught us in
the dream to help us understand its meaning. Prophet's
ability to teach us in both the dream state and waking
state is the key to our opportunity for spiritual growth.*

During a class at the Nature Awareness
School I had a dream that seemed simple at first
but was full of images that were meaningful to
me. Even a few moments of a dream can contain
a profound message from the Divine. In the
dream I was standing in the sleeping loft of a
cabin, looking down into the kitchen below. A
woman was frying two eggs and I was upset
because I did not think she should. Then I saw
Del, who is God's Prophet and my spiritual
teacher, carrying a tray of breadcrumbs outside.
Seeing Del in the dream got my attention;
seeing him is always significant. When I shared

the dream the next morning Del helped me see how this seemingly simple dream contained a key to spiritual growth.

In the loft with the higher view was Soul, my true self. As often happens in dreams the woman in the kitchen was also me, but the lower, human side of me. Through the eggs the dream showed me that my actions nourished my lower physical self, but not Soul, my higher eternal self. Like the body needs food, so does Soul. Whatever draws one closer to or into alignment with God nourishes Soul. It could be singing HU, a love song to God, practicing gratitude, reading scripture, or being aware of Prophet with me spiritually throughout the day.

However, thoughts of fear, worry, or self-doubt do not nourish us but instead drain our energy and deplete us. That is what Soul, the real eternal me, did not want my lower self to do. Yet I did often listen to my worries and fears. By doing so I could not hear God or God's Prophet whispering a solution to each of my concerns. My thoughts depleted me, affected the quality of my life, and even jeopardized an opportunity for spiritual growth.

The breadcrumbs Del carried outside were all that remained of a spiritual feast; even the opportunity for crumbs could slip away. Every class is a golden opportunity for Soul to learn and grow that comes, not once in a lifetime but once in many lifetimes. Without nourishment, Soul cannot learn and grow. I could not go any further until I learned to control my thoughts and focus on what nourishes Soul.

It would have been easy to overlook this dream and not bother to write it down or share it. It seemed so simple, yet the message was significant and of great importance to me.

Written By Jean Enzbrenner

13

Little Bird of Fear

*Sometimes upon awakening you may not remember
the specifics of a dream but know you had one. Often
the memories will return if you still make the effort to
write what little you do remember*

One morning I woke from a dream. Upon waking I could not recall specifics of the dream so I decided to just begin writing. I started with, "I dreamed…" I found as I started to write the dream slowly started to come back to me and the more I wrote, the more I remembered. It was a long dream and in it I was searching for my friend whom I had gotten separated from. I paused for a moment and was contemplating the meaning of this dream when a thought or voice came to me, which said, "When there is a brain injury, you can't fly." At the time I understood this to mean when there is fear you cannot spiritually, as Soul, go into the higher worlds or truly be yourself.

Hearing this triggered the recall of another dream I had the same night. In this dream I found a bird lying on its back. He was injured and could not fly. I picked him up and was very careful not to injure him more. I gently cupped him in my hands and sent love and encouragement. I told the little bird he would get better and fly again, which he did. As I wrote this dream in my journal it reminded me of an actual experience I had just the week before. A small bird flew into my home and got trapped inside. My cat went after him and the bird was full of fear. He flew into a closed window very hard and fell to the ground. Picking him up, I carried him outside but he was paralyzed with fear and could not fly. While holding him in my hands I encouraged him and told him he would be all right. After about ten minutes the little bird flew away.

I knew in that moment God was communicating very directly to me through my dreams. I am the friend I was separated from in the first dream. Over the years I had lost the real me while trying to fit in to please others out of fear. I am that little bird learning to fly once again.

Written by Nancy Cumpston

14

An Abundant Beautiful Life

What a gift to be shown the areas we can grow in and the things in our life that no longer serve us. Whether it is an old attitude, or a way of seeing or doing things, Prophet is here to help you clean out the clutter and manifest more joy and abundance in your life.

A number of years ago I was starting an exciting new job as a state park employee. Prior to being hired, I volunteered and assisted the Environmental Educator in implementing a series of outdoor educational programs offered to local schools. As a result of volunteering, my duties as a new state park employee were already familiar to me, and they included teaching segments of this program and to maintain and improve the facilities where these programs were conducted. These facilities included a recently renovated old barn located in a more remote gated area of the park.

The weekend before reporting to work at my new job, I attended a spiritual retreat at the Nature Awareness School. It was a beautiful early fall weekend and when class was over on the first evening Del, the Prophet of God and our spiritual teacher, suggested to the class that we ask the Divine for a dream before falling off to sleep that night. I followed his suggestion and was blessed with this incredible dream.

In the dream I was at the State Park of my upcoming new job. I was walking along the dirt road that led to the barn where programs were conducted. The gate to this area was closed so I unlatched the gate, swung it wide open, walked through, and continued on my journey following the dirt road. Upon approaching the barn I opened the door and stood in the doorway viewing the dimly lit interior. I gazed upon old junk inside that needed to be cleaned out and discarded. Mixed in with the old junk were many wonderful items worthy of keeping, one being a beautiful leather couch. I then eagerly started the task of cleaning the barn out by removing the old junk.

Upon sharing this dream with the class the next day it was suggested that the dirt road represented my spiritual journey. To continue on my spiritual journey, my heart, represented by the gate, must be open. The inside of the barn represented my life. Not much light was shining in at this particular time and the old junk piled up in the barn represented aspects of my life that no longer served me. There were, however, good items, good aspects of my life definitely worth keeping. My eagerness to start the task of cleaning out the barn showed I was ready and able to start the process of making positive changes in my life. After more class discussion on this dream, Del suggested I ask the inner Prophet for guidance in cleaning out this barn, in cleaning up aspects of my life that no longer served me. Prophet knew what was worth keeping and what I no longer needed in my life. I agreed to follow his suggestion.

Upon returning home from this class, I literally found myself at my new job at the State Park performing the task of cleaning out the exact same barn that was in my dream. It was a beautiful fall day and I was physically sorting items into piles, some worth keeping and some to be discarded. As I performed this task, my thoughts were on Prophet and I thought how absolutely amazing he is. He blesses us with outer experiences that reinforce our inner experiences. These wondrous experiences are tailor-made specifically for us.

Several years passed. I continued attending spiritual classes taught by Del at the Nature Awareness School, slowly learning to listen and follow God's inner guidance, delivered through His Prophet, to the best of my ability in all aspects of my life. Prophet can help by offering inner guidance only if I am able to listen and hear his voice, to hear and understand the "Language of the Divine" that is lovingly taught by Del. I learned that singing HU, a love song to God on a daily basis, spiritually nourishes me and tunes me in to hear and respond to Prophet's inner guidance. This inner guidance blesses me with a joyful, loving, and abundant life.

There is more. Amazingly, several years later Prophet blessed me with Part Two of the barn dream. In this dream I walked along the same dirt road as in the first dream and up to the gate, which is now wide open. I continued along on my journey following the dirt road until I came to the barn. I walked up, stood in the doorway of the barn, and viewed the interior. Beautiful golden sun light, God's Love, was brightly pouring into the barn. All that was in view were a few cobwebs and piles of old hay my family was helping me to clean up. As I recorded this dream in my dream journal, I knew immediately this dream was a continuation of my first barn dream from several years earlier. In this second dream, my heart represented by the gate, is no longer closed but is wide open to God's Love and guidance. The barn, bright with golden sunlight, is God's Love shining brightly in my life! All the piles of old junk representing old habits and negative thought processes in my dream of several years earlier are gone. My family is with me, supporting and helping me clean out those last few cobwebs and piles of old hay.

During the several year process of learning to listen to and follow Prophet's guidance and suggestions in my life, he gently awakened me to old habits and negative thought processes no longer serving me. They are gone. Incredible positive changes occurring in my life since the first barn dream are represented in the second dream. Prophet is always with me, guiding me, showering me with God's Love and helping me live an abundant, beautiful life. God's Love is definitely shining brightly in my life.

Written by Donna Hospodar

Awake Dreams

God can reach out to you in a nighttime dream while you sleep or even during the day when fully awake. When this happens during the waking state it is called an "Awake Dream." Both types of dreams can guide, protect, comfort, teach, and bless you. Awake dreams are also known as signs, coincidences, or synchronicities. It is when you, the observer, feel there is more to an experience than the surface meaning. This is the key to recognizing something as an awake dream: when your heart recognizes an event as out of the ordinary, special, or possibly containing more meaning than only the surface meaning.

Sometimes the awake dream will manifest through the spoken word, such as a song on the radio or a piece of the conversation of a passer-by just at the right time. An awake dream may also manifest as the written word, such as a billboard, license plate, or bumper sticker on a passing car. God can and will use just about anything to deliver the message to you. The common denominator of recognizing something as an awake dream is that it catches your attention and stands out to your consciousness. It gives that feeling of "what was that all about?" or "the timing of that was interesting, is there more to it?"

Most of the time an awake dream will relate to your immediate thoughts and actions. When you perceive an awake dream ask yourself, what was I just doing or thinking about? Are you considering looking for a new job or are you struggling with a relationship? If no answer comes, let it go for the time being. It is not worth spending all day on.

An important point to mention is awake dreams are not as dependable as inner communication or knowingness. The biggest danger with awake dreams is getting too "mental" trying to decipher them. For the most part you should not make a major life decision based on a single awake dream, or nighttime dream for that matter. They should merely confirm what your heart already knows to be true. You are Soul and Soul knows truth. Your "truth detector" trumps all – awake dreams included. If everything and every sign is pointing you to take a certain direction, but your heart is drawn somewhere else, follow your heart!

15

Guided to My Chiropractor

God can bless every area of our life. Nothing is "too small" to receive help with. The following is one such example of daily guidance from the Divine.

I woke up one morning with lower back pain and wanted to go to my chiropractor to get an adjustment. I thought, "It's Monday, he'll probably be too busy today." So I dismissed getting the adjustment I needed.

I proceeded with my morning routine and then drove the kids to school. After taking the kids to school I drove back home. I got out of the car and headed toward the house when I noticed a business card on the gravel in the driveway. I picked it up and adjusted the faded card so I could read it. It was the chiropractor's business card!

I knew this was Divine Spirit's way of communicating with me! I listened to this message and proceeded to go to the chiropractor that same morning. He adjusted my back and I continue to feel great! The chance of finding his card right in my path (in my line of vision) was more than a coincidence. It was a gift from God. God cares about my well-being and sent me the encouragement to get the help I needed. I am very grateful.

Written by Moira Cervone

16

God's Light Shines on a Friend's Car

If someone has the "eyes to see," they will recognize when Spirit is trying to get a message through to them. This guidance can come in unlimited ways from unlimited sources throughout your day. It might be very dramatic, but in most cases it is very subtle. Learning to become aware of these communications is an art form.

Early one morning at work I was in the staff lunch room putting my lunch in the refrigerator. My sight was drawn to a yellow light glowing in the parking lot. It was illuminated unusually bright. First, I wondered if someone left their car's parking lights on, but I saw the rest of the lights on the car were off, so that was not the case. Second, I noticed the sun was rising from the east over the hill and perhaps was at a perfect angle to illuminate this one light. Third, I took in the scene a bit more and noticed the car belonged to a friend who works with me. These three things caught my attention and caused me to wonder if there was a message in there for me. I felt a nudge to check in with my friend whose parked car was glowing with light.

In the course of the morning I had a chance to stop by her office, say hello, and ask how her weekend was. As she turned to greet me it was evident from her troubled facial expression that something was concerning her. She welcomed me in and within a few moments asked if she could speak with me confidentially.

She shared about three concerns and worries she had experienced over the weekend with three different family members. She had listened to each of the individual family issues to the best of her ability, but felt badly for each one and the tough times they have to go through. She could not let go of their fear, worry, and anger discussed over the weekend. As she shared she saw more clearly that the emotions she was wearing were not hers to wear. She realized that there was only so much she could do for her family, and the rest was their responsibility to work through, not hers. She was gaining insight into being supportive and then knowing when to step back and surrender the outcome. Her willingness to share helped relieve her worries. She said she felt better, now able to face the busy day ahead at work. I could clearly see the stress that was so evident minutes before had lifted. Her facial expression now relaxed, she looked like herself again.

Reflecting on this experience I learned Divine Spirit is always talking to me. It catches my attention in any way it can to help me be receptive to Its message. The Light of God illuminated a parking light on a friend's car at a very precise time that morning so I would see It! The Light of God shed Its understanding on a friend's heart, bringing peace to her so she could move forward with her responsibilities at work. Paying attention to the guidance of Divine Spirit and following Its nudges that morning helped to strengthen my inner communication with the Voice of God.

Written by Ann Atwell

17

Bay Leaves Bring Romantic Cabin for Two

Guidance from God can come in many ways and be about any part of our life. Sometimes it can be very obvious, sometimes very subtle. The key is being aware and learning to trust what your heart knows to be true, regardless of what anyone else says.

In the summer of 2013 my husband Mark and I were planning a weeklong vacation in Houghton Lake, Michigan to visit friends and family. We currently live in Virginia so all our searching had to be done on the internet. We found a listing "Romantic Cabin for Two" that looked promising, but it was twenty minutes away from my aunt's house. My aunt thought we should rent a cabin that was across the street from her. Which to pick? It was hard to decide if we should be closer to her or enjoy the nicer lake getaway. I asked my inner guide, the Prophet, for help and then went about the day.

While at the store shopping the next day I was cruising an isle of spices when a bag of bay leaves caught my eye. I picked it up and opened the twist tie to inhale the rich aroma of the leaves. They smelled wonderful. Even though I did not need them I put them in the cart. Later that night I was looking at a map of Houghton Lake to see exactly where the cabin we liked was in relation to my aunt's house. I discovered it was located on the bay. Then I realized my strong attraction to the bay leaves was telling me to stick with my original choice, the cabin on the bay.

I shared this awake dream during my first Dream Retreat at the Nature Awareness School. The teacher, Del Hall IV, helped me see a pearl of wisdom in this experience. He asked the question, "What if the bay leaves meant to leave the bay?" (Bay-LEAVE). I took a moment to check how I felt. He told me not to change my answer. He reminded me to follow my heart when interpreting an awake dream. Awake dreams most often are confirmations of what we already know to be true.

Mark and I decided to book the romantic cabin. I attended the Dream Retreat before I went on vacation so this was a good opportunity to test my "truth detector," something I learned about at the Nature Awareness School. We all have one; it is a blessing from God that helps me to navigate through life. It allows me to know truth when I hear it and has been strengthened as I have learned to trust my inner communication from the Prophet.

Sure enough, when Mark and I pulled up the gravel drive to the bayside cabin our jaws were dropping. The entire place inside and out was put together with so much love. It was more beautiful than the pictures online. Even my aunt, who was originally disappointed by our decision, said we made the right choice.

God can use anything, even a bay leaf, to get a message across if we are receptive to His Voice. We can ask God for help. There is no issue too small. If it is important to us, it is important to God. We are Soul and as such God has given us the ability to receive His guidance. This inner communication is my lifeline. Knowing that God is still active and guiding me has made my life such a joy to live. We are never alone!

Written by Carmen Snodgrass

18

God Blesses Four Generations

Great story highlighting many of the ways God can communicate with you and the blessings that come from listening.

I am very grateful to have been raised in a family that recognizes and values communication with God. My father taught me from a very young age that God communicates with His children in many ways and to pay attention to my sleeping dreams, "coincidences," and inner nudges from the Divine. My father also taught me I am not alone, that I am heard, and that everything from my daily walk through life to my inner most dreams is important to God. I would like to share how knowing about the various ways God communicates with me has blessed interactions with my daughter, grandmother, and mother.

One weekend my seven-year-old daughter was getting frustrated with my five-year-old daughter. She did not want to play with her, which is okay, but the way she told her to go away hurt her sister's feelings. She had also been slightly rude to me the night before when I arrived to pick her up from her after-school program. That Saturday she stubbed her toe at least four times in the matter of a few hours. It struck me that something was out of the ordinary and there might be a Divine message in the repeated injuries. I was singing the HU song silently to myself, and I asked on the inner for guidance as to what the message might be. The answer I heard was that it was an awake dream tied to her hurting people's feelings.

I do not think my seven-year-old was trying to hurt anyone's feelings, but she did, just like she did not mean to stub her toe, but it still hurt. I was able to share with her the message I thought she was being given and she understood. We also discussed how stubbing her toe could become part of her personal waking dream language (symbols that can recur and develop a special meaning and therefore make communication with the Divine even more fluent). In the future if she stubs her toe she might pause and look to see if she may have hurt someone's feeling inadvertently. It might just be a stubbed toe however, and if she listens to God with her heart she will know the difference. Being a typical seven-year-old she asked if she could change the awake dream symbol to rose petals on the ground, which was pretty funny but not likely. Knowing God is in my life and can help me to be a better parent is amazing.

Here is another example of hearing a message from the Divine. Shortly before my grandmother passed away I overheard at least three people in one day having conversations about their grandmothers having recently passed away. The multiple references to losing a grandmother and my own grandmother's declining health gave me the nudge to call her. I listened to the insight and called her and told her that I loved her, and even mentioned a few of my special childhood memories to her. I did not want to frighten her, so I used discretion and did not tell her that I was calling to say goodbye. She did end up passing away shortly after I called. It was a huge gift from God that I had been able to express my love for her one last time in the physical.

My love for my grandmother transcends the physical, as does my love connection with my mother. One of my personal awake dream symbols is a red cardinal. This particular awake dream relates to my mother who passed away when I was sixteen years old. Over the years I noticed that when I was thinking about her or missing her I would see a red cardinal. The cardinal would usually land on a branch directly in my view and then once I got the message fly away. To me the bird represents the love connection my mother and I still have even though she is no longer with me in the physical. Every time I see a red cardinal it is not necessarily an awake dream, some are just birds. I know in my heart when it is a message because it is always perfectly timed to when I am sending her love or wishing I could talk to her.

Written by Catherine Hughes

19

Pink Carnations

God expresses His Love for us every day. Often this Love goes unrecognized because God communicates in many different and often subtle ways. Once you become more fluent in the "Language of the Divine" you will recognize this love all around you.

My father's favorite flowers were pink carnations. He really loved them. When he passed away in September of 2012, my mother made the decision to not have a funeral or share any announcements of his passing. One day he was in the hospital, and then he is just gone.

Two months later I was attending a spiritual retreat at the Nature Awareness School. I had gone upstairs to use the restroom. There, sitting on the sink vanity, was a bouquet of beautiful pink carnations. I stood there for a bit and cried. I knew these flowers were a gift from God. It was God's way of letting me know everything was fine with my dad. He is okay. These flowers brought relief, peace, joy, and comfort to my heart. God knew how much my heart was hurting and that I really missed my dad. This awake dream was a gift of love from God. Thank you God for your love and comfort.

Written By Rebecca Vettorel

20

Prayer Averts Health Problem

Our prayers are heard but it is up to us to recognize the answer.

About twelve years ago, shortly after I moved to Virginia, I noticed my overall health was declining. I found myself more and more tired, moody, and irritable. I had wondered if a food I was eating could be causing my symptoms, but I was unable to determine the exact cause. After several unsuccessful months of trying to figure out what was going on, I received some help from Spirit that changed my life.

One evening after work I decided to make pancakes and eggs for dinner. After mixing up the pancake batter I let it sit for a moment and I sat myself on the couch to rest. I relaxed for a moment then began singing HU to express my love for God. I asked God to please help me figure out what was going on with my body. After a few minutes I got up to make my pancakes. As I walked into the kitchen, the box of pancake mix fell off the counter and its contents spilled on the floor. Cleaning up the mess I wondered, "What is going on, boxes of pancake mix don't just jump off the counter." As I picked the box of pancake mix off the floor the ingredients list was turned towards me. In big bold letters the word WHEAT seemed to be highlighted and almost jumping off the box. Kneeling on the floor with this box in my hand, staring at those bold letters I wondered, "Maybe I'm allergic to wheat? Is this an answer to my prayer?"

A few days later I followed through on the insight I had been given. I started looking for a doctor, and after being tested for several allergens, she concluded I was indeed allergic to wheat. During the testing she also found I had high levels of lead in my blood. After I eliminated the allergens from my diet and cleansed the lead out of my body, my health improved greatly. I am very grateful to have been given this awake dream, which led to a major improvement in my health.

Written by Mark Snodgrass

21

God's Golden Scissors
Give Freedom

It is one thing to do something nice for someone you love. It is quite another if you become overly attached to pleasing them. This excessive attachment becomes entangling and it leads to stress, a lack of peace, deluding yourself, and ultimately not following your heart. Of all the things that cause Soul unrest, not following one's heart is near the top of the list. Fortunately the Prophet can gently help untangle those who are under his wing from their attachments so they can live with more freedom.

Have you ever been tangled up in a situation and not been sure how to get yourself out? I certainly have and by the Grace of God, I was given an experience that helped free me from my attachments to an unhealthy relationship in my life. I entangled myself in a web that held me back from fully following my heart. The worst part about it was that I was deluding myself. I was attached to pleasing someone else and was not honest about my true motivations. This entanglement was causing stress in my life. Thank God that He sends His ordained Prophet into this world to help us see and understand truths about life. While a major part of the Prophet's responsibility lies in guiding us home in the Heavenly Worlds, he also teaches and demonstrates how to live a freer and more balanced life here on Earth: a blessing with practical benefits.

During Christmas several years ago God was giving me signs, all through my life, that something was amiss. I was making poor choices and overextending myself. I was not living true to the priorities in my heart. In an effort to please a member of my extended family I was compromising my overall balance. Adding to my struggle, in the midst of this busy time, I badly hurt my back. This is when God's Grace stepped in to help me help myself. I was at a weekend retreat at the Nature Awareness School. There the loving guidance and presence of my teacher, Del Hall, began to untangle this web. As the current Prophet he has special training to communicate with and teach both in the physical and in the inner spiritual worlds. Del could clearly sense something was amiss. One of the many blessings of being a student of Prophet is that he can help clear our vision and show us areas where we are entangled or limiting ourselves, if we give permission. I needed help and he lovingly helped me get to the root of what was going on.

The opportunity to share some of our life experiences during a class gives Del the chance to share his inner insights with us. From what he shared it was clear this relationship with my family member was negatively affecting all of my other relationships, including my relationship with God. For anyone who has ever had an unhealthy relationship, be it with a husband or wife, sibling, friend, co-worker, etc., the need to "make it better" is sometimes overwhelming and counter-productive. I was choosing to compromise my peace in an effort to appease this person.

Excessive attachment is one of the most insidious passions that can harm us on our path home to God. Often it comes cloaked in a good thing, like wanting to fix something we deem broken, but true peace is being right with God. Putting our relationship with God first brings peace to the other areas of our lives. On the other hand, repeatedly choosing to live without peace in one area of our lives negatively affects all other areas as well. The truth was this relationship with a family member was unhealthy for me. Part of the healing process is facing the truth and accepting it, then making conscious choices that nurture the healing we have received.

On Sunday morning of the retreat we sang HU. I had surrendered what I was going through to the Divine, had asked for help, and now I was focused on singing "I love you" to God. Afterward it was quiet in the room. God blessed me with a clarity and stillness that had been missing in my life for weeks. In my inner vision an aspect of God gave me a pair of golden scissors. I immediately knew the function and purpose of this gift was to cut away my attachment to this unhealthy relationship. As I began to cut I could see other attachments and cut those cords as well. Now free of these self-imposed webs that had been entangling me, I began to experience true freedom. A well of love sprang forth from my heart. I realized what I had thought before was love was nowhere close to the real thing. This was a degree of unconditional love I had yet to experience giving to another person. I felt so free. To truly wish someone well and not be attached to what that looks like is a purer love. These scissors were real. This gift from God transformed me from the inside out and began a deep change in my life that continues to bless me today.

I received further confirmation of my decision when I returned home. My five-year-old son had drawn me a picture while I was away. In it there were two ships. One was a pirate ship and the other was a smiley face ship. Under the water strings, cords, and ropes attached the two ships. There were three pairs of scissors. My son had never even drawn scissors before! The scissors were cutting the ropes to the pirate ship, but the smiley face ship still had one cord that connected it to the bottom of the ocean.

This awake dream gave me further reassurance I was making the right choice in cutting these unhealthy attachments. God's truth was demonstrated in the simplicity of a child's drawing. I could cut this unhealthy relationship from my life, choose to stay anchored in God's unconditional Love, and live life with more freedom.

Written by Molly Comfort

Healing

You could make the case that on one level all dreams should be considered healing. They all are a reminder of God's guiding Hand and Love. For the sake of organizing this book to show the value and importance of dreams, this section deals specifically with healings: emotional, mental, physical, or spiritual. There are also times when one knows they have received a healing but does not know the specifics. They awake with an unknown "block" or "heaviness" removed. Whatever area the healing covers, all healings are ultimately a gift of love from God.

Sometimes a healing may be dramatic and at other times it may be very subtle. The healing may come immediately in the dream. Other times the dreamer receives information or clarity on which way to move forward (such as being led to the right doctor) to manifest the healing.

Physical healing, while perhaps the most thought of, is only temporal. To be healed of the things holding you back spiritually is potentially a permanent healing. If God's Prophet removes something blocking you from experiencing more of God's Love and truth, such as anger, vanity, fear, lust, or undue attachments, it pays dividends not only this life, but in all future existence. Our receptiveness also plays a part in our ability to receive a healing, and it is our responsibility to nurture these gifts of healing to maintain them.

22

Broken Heart Healed in a Dream

Sometimes by simply showing us the truth in a dream God sets us free. The following is a beautiful example of someone being at the point where they are receptive to truth, no matter what it is, and the dramatic emotional healing that followed.

Fifteen years ago I had an emotional healing in a dream I still thank God for today. My boyfriend of four years had finally ended our tempestuous, fight-filled relationship, and while I was in many ways relieved, the separation was agony. I spent a lot of time fantasizing that someday, in a few years after I had improved myself by learning Spanish and gaining a Master's Degree he would take me back. It was a silly fantasy, but it was about the only thing that cheered me enough to eat – otherwise I was too sad to have an appetite. I went on like this for about six weeks, crying half the time, fantasizing about an eventual reunion the other half. My ex-boyfriend and I still spoke on the phone about once a week, at my begging, and I would sort of work on him, half asking him to take me back, half mourning our breakup. I was not moving on, and I was preventing him from doing so as well. My pain was not improving; time was not healing my broken heart.

During all this, my sister asked me to visit her and help out while she had her third baby. It was a change of scene but I continued to suffer. One night I told my sister the whole story about the breakup, crying my eyes out the whole time. After that I went to my bedroom, took out my journal, and wrote to God. I told Him I wanted to make a good life, a life of service to Him. I told God I wanted clarity and direction, and I asked God, "Please just let me see what is going to happen with this relationship. Are we going to get back together or what? I just want to know." Then I went to sleep.

In the morning, right before it was time to wake up, I had a vivid dream. I was up at my family's vacation place on a remote lake in Canada using the phone booth at the little marina. I was making a call to my ex-boyfriend in the States, but it was a tricky thing because of my remote location. Space aliens were helping connect the signal and finally I spoke with him. "I can't do this anymore!" he shouted over the weak connection. "That's okay," I shouted back, "I can't either!" And that was it. I woke up, and I was healed. I was completely over the relationship. Not angry, not sad, not regretful. Just past it. I could almost detect a physical soreness, as one would feel after surgery, but the previous deep pain was completely removed overnight. I knew it was a healing from God. The bonus was that I had also received a quiet knowing that I would in time meet the right person. I did not know when, but God would send me the right guy, perfect for me.

This dream God gave me was an opportunity for my ex-boyfriend and me to speak Soul to Soul and communicate our deepest truths, something that had not been possible for us to do in the physical world. The truth was I did not want the relationship at all, and God let me see it plainly.

The rest of the visit with my sister was beautiful. More than just feeling better, I also enjoyed knowing I had received a deep, spiritual healing from God – a true miracle. How amazing to have all that heartbreak lifted in one night. To know God loves me that much. I wondered with excitement and gratitude about what was to come.

Fifteen years later I still marvel at the amazing dream and the Divine healing it delivered. I do not think it would have happened if I had not totally surrendered to God when I wrote that note in my journal. I simply asked God for the truth. I did not tell Him what to do; really I just asked for help, whatever that looked like. The help God sent was not in a form I might have expected – it was even better than I could have imagined.

Written by Joan Clickner

23

A Year of Healing Dreams

*Sometimes the circumstances of a relationship that
ends do not afford us the opportunity to speak in
person afterwards and come to a place of closure and
healing. Fortunately, God can bring us together
spiritually in dreams to resolve any remaining issues,
heal our wounds, and move forward with peace.*

After the end of a difficult relationship with
someone I loved but was not able to live with
anymore, I had a series of healing dreams. These
dreams made it possible for both of us to forgive
one another and move on to healthier and
happier lives.

We had been together for eight years and
had acquired property together. Deciding to
end our relationship was the last resort. We tried
counseling, life coaching workshops, and other
means to heal our relationship. None of that
worked. The love was still there but there was no
more trust. A betrayal had made it impossible to
continue our partnership. Although I knew that I

needed to move out and move on, I could not seem to shake the guilt and sadness of this break up. We were not able to communicate with each other after the trust was gone and still to this day have not had contact in the physical. I began to pray to God for help so I could move on and heal. That night I had an experience on the inner planes during a dream. It was very vivid and real.

This Soul and I were in a vast open desert world and we were in our light bodies. We still had our human forms, but the bodies were made of sparkling light. We were facing one another and a great wave of love cascaded between us. No words were spoken. I woke up from this experience and felt much more at peace about our decision. I had less guilt and had insights into how we accomplished what we were meant to in our relationship in this lifetime. For the first time, I did not feel like we had wasted all those years. Everything seemed in perfect order and right on schedule.

During the course of that year I had several similar dreams. I eventually had a dream that showed me the original cause of our need to go through this difficult experience together, which happened in another lifetime. From time to time I still have dreams with this Soul and we are able to speak kindly to one another. The strong emotions and attachments are gone. We genuinely wish one another well.

Many years after this series of healing dreams I got validation of what my heart knew to be true during classes at the Nature Awareness School. I realized we had indeed both had a healing. They did not happen in my mind, they were very real. I know that as messy as all of it looked, it was perfect. Old karma was resolved between us, and I had gained wisdom and a greater capacity to love, which I brought into my new relationship. The series of inner experiences (dreams) and the understanding of them led to closure in what might have been an endless pattern of pain between two Souls. I am very grateful.

Written by Tash Canine

24

God's Healing Love

God's Love gives us life and we are never without it. We were created from and continue to be nourished by His Light and Love. This love also has the power to heal us: spiritually, mentally, and physically. There is no ill that the Love of God cannot soothe.

One morning I awoke early feeling quite poorly with a headache accompanied by nausea. Since I worked the afternoon shift I decided there was sufficient time to allow the sick feeling to go away on its own instead of taking medication. Several hours passed without any relief. I decided to prepare for a short nap with a spiritual practice that brings me peace and comfort. I opened my heart and expressed love and appreciation to God by singing HU, then went to sleep. HU is a love song to God taught to me by Prophet Del Hall III, my spiritual teacher.

While I was asleep I had a dream of being bathed in a beautiful and comforting golden light. Upon awakening the symptoms of my illness were completely gone. Gratitude for the healing Light of God's Love overtook me while I realized how much I am loved and cared for.

Prophet has taught me how to fortify my awareness of the connection that exists between God and me. He has helped me recognize that the personal love connection I have with the Divine is the most precious bond I will ever have.

Written by Bernadette Spitale

25

Healed of Guiltiness

*God does not want us living in guilt – for any reason.
Guilt breeds unworthiness, which pushes away love.
Unfortunately, it is very common for folks to have some
level of guilt after someone close to them passes away.
Thankfully, a loving God can provide us with the
healing we need to move on and open our hearts more
fully to love.*

I was asked in a retreat at the Nature Awareness School, "What is the first dream you remember?" I immediately recalled a dream experience I had over twenty years ago. I know it was real and a gift from the Divine meant specifically for me.

To earn extra money to put myself through college, I held a job cleaning elderly people's homes through an agency called Office of the Aging. This appealed to me because ever since I was a young girl I always seemed to have an older and wiser woman in my life. At this time, I was without one. The agency soon ended this program, but I remained with Antonia for four years. I would tidy up her home and take her clothes to the Laundromat, but mostly I would listen. She shared with me about living in her country, Latvia, and then immigrating to the United States. I enjoyed Antonia and she held a very special place in my heart and life.

During the time I was taking final exams, life became very busy, and I had not seen or talked to Antonia for a few weeks. When I called her she did not answer her phone. I even knocked on her apartment door, but there was no answer. I soon read her obituary in the paper. I felt a great loss in her passing, and I now know that God knew I was very, very sad. Soon after I was given a dream and Antonia appeared to me. She appeared as a very large beautiful white light standing over and above me. She spoke and said that she is just fine and all is okay. We were given a moment together, which was engraved into my heart as we shared our hearts with one another. As I apologized to her she lovingly waved her hand as if erasing all the guilt I was burdened by and said a few more comforting things to me.

Her presence revealed a message for me not to be sad but to move on with my life and to be happy. She was obviously happy, which was wonderful to see because in her physical life she was often sad and struggled with depression. When I awoke, I was immediately and instantly freed from any guilt I put upon myself for not being with her when she passed on. This Divine experience changed what I thought I knew or felt at that time about death. It helped me to know and believe we are eternal, we do not die, and I have nothing to be afraid of.

This real experience also lit a spark within me. It opened me up to adventurously seeking God and gave me a sense that there is so much more to God's Love. I absolutely know God was reading my heart, healing me, comforting me, and giving me the solace I was craving. I also knew Antonia was in God's Hands. With all of what I experienced, I was given the gifts of being freed, healed, comforted, and left with a knowing that God is truly real and heard my cry.

I was given an experience that healed me and gave me a new perspective of life. I went from being grief-stricken and stuck to being uplifted and freed. Yes, what a dream to remember! I am so appreciative of the Presence of God in my heart, in my life, and in my dreams.

Written by Moira Cervone

26

A Healing Banquet

Often the things causing us a lack of peace or holding us back have their origins in a prior lifetime. Our mind may not consciously remember the experiences, but we still carry the hurt. When light is shined on the true root cause healing can begin in earnest.

"Thou preparest a table before me in the presence of mine enemies"   Psalm 23 KJV

God has the ability to bring us together in dreams to resolve the issues of the past, those that hinder our spiritual progress. I had the following dream while attending a class at the Nature Awareness School.

I was at a large banquet. About forty to fifty people sat at a large oaken banquet table filled with an abundance of food. These were Souls I had incarnated with in a previous life. Everyone appeared as they looked in their previous life. A comfortable familiarity existed between us, our love connections continuing as if no time had passed. Other Souls began to arrive and join us at the table. Each of these individuals had caused harm to one or more Souls already seated. It was as if the verse from the twenty-third Psalm came to life. The Lord had indeed prepared a table for me in the presence and company of my enemies. Yet they were here for the truth also. There was no preference for anyone injured over those who had caused harm. There were no victims here. All were simply God's children looking to heal so they could move forward spiritually in *this* life. This was an amazing opportunity for me to experience and witness. Truth and acceptance are a powerful combination. Forgiveness of self and others is often the byproduct.

I too had the opportunity to confront someone now seated beside me. Anger and unforgiveness welled up within me, yet I was moved with deep compassion as I saw the openness and sincerity in this Soul's eyes. He genuinely wanted to understand what harm he might have caused. I pulled back my shirt to show him scars on my chest. These might have been literal scars from that lifetime, or it may have been symbolic of the anger and unforgiveness I still carried from our encounter.

Suddenly I heard a soothing voice. I felt reassured and calmed as my body became immobilized. I felt safe and free to relive this familiar experience. Suffocating in my sleep was a recurring nightmare from my childhood. I would often yell and scream as I struggled for what felt like hours to wake. I often woke to find my physical body completely relaxed and breathing normally. Now having been taken to the root cause, there was no longer any need to experience it further. I relived this one last time and by the healing Grace of God have been free of it ever since.

There is only so much room in our hearts. Prophet has taught me that our choices and our responses decide in large part what we allow into it. Dreams are one way God can bring awareness to these matters and lead us to acceptance, and ultimately, healing and freedom. This one experience has brought me greater peace in the form of more forgiveness, compassion, and freedom. I am grateful for this blessing!

Written by Chris Comfort

27

Precision Dream Provides Healing

Dreams can serve as a source of healing on many different levels. In the following example a dream helped the author help her doctor. She was able to translate valuable information to him, which ultimately was the cause for her healing. Why would the Divine reach out through dreams to help us? Quite simply: it is because we are loved.

I needed help with the back pain I have had since an accident in 2000, and I decided to visit a practitioner who does osteopathic techniques. After the first session he developed a treatment plan for our follow-up sessions. His plan was to work on my right hip. The night before I went to see him for my second treatment I had a dream.

In the dream I was on an exam table, and there were two people diagnosing me. They asked me to put my left leg into a figure four position. As I did this the imbalance in my pelvis became really obvious. They both commented on how severely twisted my pelvis was, and said the right illiopsoas muscle and oblique muscle were stuck in a holding pattern. Then I woke up.

I wrote the dream down. What stood out to me was the specific muscles named in the dream; I felt they had to be important if they were named. I decided to share this dream with my practitioner since he also follows dream guidance. After I told him about the dream he reviewed his notes from our first session and began working on my right hip. About ten minutes into the session he stopped and asked me to repeat the specific muscles that were in my dream. I told him and it was like a light bulb went off. He said that information actually changed everything. He needed to work on my pelvis and not my hips. He shifted the focus of his work three inches. Once he did this a lot began to happen and the work started to flow. He told me if it was not for me sharing this dream, I would not have gotten anything from the sessions. The treatment for this injury needed to be very precise, and the information I was given in my dream made that precision possible.

This is an example of how God might answer a prayer for help. Many times we are led to a doctor or a specific type of treatment through dreams. In my case, I was led to the practitioner and told about the specific areas that needed attention. The Divine is always speaking to us and helping us. It is up to us to learn how to listen. Investing in understanding my personal dream language has paid off many times. It has helped me understand more about God's Love, including how to have a relationship with the Divine through this skill set.

I see this dream and the healing that resulted as a huge gift from God.

Written by Tash Canine

28

Healing Pink and Orange Light

Even though our experiences may be painful they are helping us grow in our ability to give and receive love: the greater the challenge the greater the opportunity for growth. Even though it might take years to accept or understand the lessons of our trials, they are not punishment from God. They are opportunities to grow even closer to Him.

I have been blessed with an amazing best friend since childhood. When we were in elementary school we spent every possible waking moment together. In middle school she moved about thirty minutes away and we begged our willing mothers to drive us back and forth. Then in high school I moved several states away and during college we found ourselves on opposite ends of the country. The periods of time between visits and distance between us might have been extended, but it had no diminishing effect on our friendship. Six months could pass without talking, and then with one phone call it was like there had been no separation at all. Now as adults the physical distance between us has become only a few states and we are able to see each other once or twice a year.

She has been there for me through many of my significant moments: losing my mother at the age of sixteen, getting married, and being blessed with two children. I have been there for her through many of her significant moments: losing her beloved childhood dog, her marriage, and her journey to motherhood. Since we were kids we have both dreamed of becoming mothers. We talked about different names and how many kids we hoped to have one day.

She was blessed to conceive a baby girl in 2013 and was due to deliver in June of 2014. We celebrated in the usual ways and I shared stories of my own pregnancies, sleepless days with a newborn, and how motherhood had brought about a deep love in me beyond my wildest imagination. She was on the doorstep of her dream becoming a reality. It never occurred to me that something heartbreaking would change the course of our lives. Tragically, during her delivery she lost her baby and suffered severe physical trauma to her own body. Feelings of shock, helplessness, and disbelief hit me harder than I can ever recall in this lifetime. I was hundreds of miles away when I heard the news and could not bear the feeling that I had zero power or ability to ease the pain for my dear friend and her family. I could not even imagine what she was experiencing.

I wept, prayed, and sang HU for twenty-four hours straight after hearing the news. I prayed with everything in me to God to please lift even one ounce of the pain and suffering from her heart. Slowly God showed me I was not entirely powerless. With God anything is possible, I am so grateful to know prayers are real and they provide the sacred opportunity to express our feelings directly to God. I am so grateful Prophet has given me the tools to express my compassion, and the deep trust to know we are all in God's hands. I do not know mentally why her life took this course, but I trust God, and there was a reason it did.

The first day after hearing the news my prayers were answered, and I was blessed with a dream and a spiritual visit to my friend. In the dream her baby was alive and healthy and being cared for and nurtured by two loving Souls in Heaven. I was able to hold her and feel the warmth of her soft skin. It brought me peace to know her daughter was being watched over, and hope that maybe one day this Soul could try again to become her child. The mother and child love bond they share transcends their physical separation.

Prophet also blessed me with a very real visit to my friend. Her body had been through a very traumatic experience physically and she was very weak and on bed rest. For a period of time she could not even ascend the stairs to her bedroom and had to sleep on her couch. I found myself as Soul sitting on the floor in her apartment and holding her hand while she lay on the couch. No words were spoken. The entire room was filled with a misty golden light, God's Love and Presence gently surrounding her and her family. Over her heart there was an intense pink light, which I believe to be God's healing Light; the pink color represented to me an emotional healing filled with strength, love, and hope. Over her womb there was an intense orange light which I believe represented physical healing and strength to aid in repairing the physical trauma. God's Light and Love surrounded her and held her safe and sound. It gently but intensely washed over her and through her both physically and spiritually.

Words cannot fully convey the gift this experience was and still is for me. In the year following her loss I am often taken back to this moment, and I know she is still being nurtured and cared for by Our Heavenly Father. I can support her with cards, phone calls, food, and honorary gifts in her daughter's name. Even more precious is the Divine opportunity to be able to pray to God to please, if it is His will, send strength, comfort, love, peace, healing, and even hope for a child in the future. God loves His children, and God loves when His children love one another.

My friend has again been blessed to conceive a child, this time a baby boy, due in October. He will learn all about his sister from those who love her. I am thankful to God for my lifelong friendship. I am thankful to God to know His Light is real and powerful. I am thankful to Prophet for showing me my friend being blessed with Divine Light, as it brought me peace and comfort. I am thankful to know God's Light brought a profound healing to her, whether or not she is fully aware of its magnitude.

Written by Catherine Hughes

Comfort

Life has its challenges. Ultimately they are opportunities for growth, but nonetheless the bumps in the road can be jarring. God can comfort His children through dreams, wherever they may be physically. Whether they need reassurance on a tough decision they have to make or have made, a vote of confidence they are on the right track, a reminder they are loved, and all will be well in the end, God, through His Prophet, can deliver all these gifts of comfort and love in dreams.

29

Comfort During Divorce

This is a great example of someone being comforted in a dream during a tough decision.

I had just made the decision to leave my marriage of twenty years and I was feeling very anxious and fretting. Was I doing the right thing for all the people affected in leaving my marriage? I was most concerned for my two sons. One evening before I fell asleep I asked for guidance. This is the dream that was given to me.

I was in a room with a friend and she was in a rocking chair sitting by the window knitting. I looked out the window and saw a large white eagle flying upward with a basket in his talons. My two boys were in the basket being carefully lifted upward by the white eagle. The boys appeared to be fine; they were not worried or upset.

I woke up knowing I had made the right decision. A sense of peace had replaced the anguish and worries I had been feeling. I had a deep knowing that all were in good hands. This was the right plan even though my emotions had been indicating the opposite. I knew God was taking care of the boys and this was going to help them grow.

My friend knitting in the rocking chair represented me in a peaceful and comforting state. The white eagle represented Divine Spirit, God. The eagle holding my children assured me God would be looking after them during this time. Flying upward indicated moving in an upward growth direction for the boys. Besides the comfort and reassurance I inwardly felt, I knew the prayers of my heart were heard. I had been praying for my family to be cared for and looked after during this turbulent time. I knew God had heard my prayer as our prayers are always heard. In this dream experience I was comforted by being shown and reassured that all would be well.

Written by Renée Walker

30

Moving to Virginia

Sometimes we may receive the guidance we need through a single dream. At other times we may receive a series of dreams on the same subject over a longer period of time. The following testimony is a great example of the latter.

As I reflect upon the events of the past year, my heart is filled with so much gratitude, appreciation, and love for the Prophet. My wife Michelle and I had a prayer and dream in our hearts to move from Pennsylvania to Virginia so we could be closer to the Nature Awareness School in the Blue Ridge Mountains. This involved finding a new job and moving with our three children several hundred miles. Surely we are not the first family to make such a move, but it was a big adjustment for us and there was much uncertainty about it. There were many things to consider: finances, friendships, new jobs and careers, finding a new home, and placing the kids in school. It was overwhelming to sort through all the logistical details of such a move, even though I tried in vain to do so.

I prayed many times for Divine guidance to lead me through this transition, and Prophet showed me some profound and stunning blessings. I trusted God would provide for me and my family, and He certainly did. Guidance and insights came in dreams, gentle nudges, and comforting peace. I discovered that when my heart is open and my attention focused on the Divine, I can nurture a loving connection with Prophet and through this connection the possibilities are boundless.

While there were many changes and uncertainties during this time, having a solid and loving relationship with Prophet brought so much peace, comfort, and inner confidence. Walking this journey with Prophet is such a joy and an adventure. I saw Divine love and blessings in so many things, in so many forms, down to the simplest of things. While I trust in God and His Prophet, it is also important to balance that reliance with personal effort. After all, Prophet's job is not to do it all for me. For several months I made an effort to fulfill my part of this responsibility by preparing my resume and searching for job opportunities. We researched school districts and housing markets in the area. We reviewed our finances, saved money, and contemplated on how we might go about moving. The realization that we may need to pack and load our belongings into a rental truck prompted us to sort through our possessions and donate unused items. We found it a joy to do this.

There were some twists and turns and unexpected outcomes in the journey to find a new job and place to live. I was blessed with several job interviews, and Prophet gracefully guided me through each one. I received a job offer from a reputable company, and while it was tempting to accept the job to fulfill the prayer, Prophet gave a nudge telling me it was not the right one. This job required some demanding time constraints and the company culture was not a suitable match. I would tense up with the thought of accepting the offer and would relax with thoughts of rejecting it. This was my confirmation to reject their offer. So the journey continued. More weeks passed with a couple new opportunities, and there were times I wondered if I would find a job in my field, or if I should look at exploring a new career. There were emotional ups and downs and Prophet was there with me through it all, working behind the scenes to prepare the way and gently guide me.

Just days before the Thanksgiving holiday I got a chance to interview with a company I was really excited about. The job description was a good fit and the interview went really well. Meeting with the employees confirmed this was a place I wanted to work. The company extended an offer that was better than I expected. The salary and benefits exceeded my expectations, and to my pleasant surprise, the offer included a relocation assistance package that originally was unavailable to me. The addition of this relocation assistance greatly alleviated some financial and logistical challenges of moving my family three hundred miles. What a tremendous blessing!

Next in our journey was finding a place to live, and we had a couple of short weeks between the Thanksgiving and Christmas holidays to do so. We quickly discovered this was not an optimal time to find housing. Michelle and I traveled to the area one day with the intent of meeting with a few landlords and signing a rental lease. We prayed together that morning for God to guide us to the right place. After touring a few homes none of the available options really appealed to us, but we could make one work to suit our needs. Then late in the day we found a posting that seemed really interesting. We called the phone number and made an appointment that evening. This turned out to be the place for us, and we signed a lease a short time later. Once again God answered our prayer and guided us to the home right for us.

I was given a very uplifting dream the night before we were to make the move to Virginia. Del, the Prophet, was teaching a group of students, me included, and God's Love flowed from him to all around, touching everyone and everything. Love poured through His presence and words. I awoke feeling so much love! It was wonderful. A few hours after awakening, we started driving to Virginia. As I drove closer, the feeling of God's Love intensified, giving me confirmation once again that this move was truly a gift from God.

A few days later, on the night before my first day of work, I was given another dream. Prophet spoke to me in the dream and said he has been teaching me for years to follow the blue light, which is symbolic of Prophet's presence. We were then immersed in a beautiful blue light as we continued our conversation. Along with the blue light I had a strong feeling of God's Love and protection that stayed with me even after I awoke. As I rose from bed and started my day, I was surprised at how little anxiety I felt about starting a new job. I was at peace with what I was doing and relaxed despite the uncertainties that lay ahead. I was confident in the Lord that this is where I was supposed to be.

In hindsight I can see how this job is the perfect one for me, better than the other positions I pursued. Prophet loves me and knows precisely what is in my best interest. I can see how Prophet has prepared me for several years to not just do this job, but have a chance to really excel at it. There are opportunities for me to grow and thrive and touch others by sharing Divine love.

I am also extremely grateful because our children embraced the move and adapted remarkably well to the transition. It is obvious that Prophet prepared them on the inner for this journey and comforted them along the way. They did not resist; in fact they were really excited about it and seemed to enjoy it. They did well in their new school and found new friends quickly. Sharing this experience as a family brought us closer together and strengthened our love for each other.

I am certainly blessed to have the dreams in my heart answered beyond my best imagination. It is by the Grace of God that I am living happily with my family in Virginia near the Nature

Awareness School. Prophet prepared my family and I in many ways for a long time to accept this opportunity and fulfill the dreams in our hearts. God hears our prayers and wants to bless all areas of our life with abundance, if we are willing to open our hearts and make room for Divine love.

Written by Chris Hibshman

31

Inner Knowing Trumps Technology

You do not "have" a Soul - you "are" Soul. This is a simple but profound change in perspective. One of Soul's attributes is the ability to communicate with the Divine through an inner guide or teacher. The following is a great example of how this can bless your daily life.

On most evenings before bed I speak with my girlfriend on the phone. We both appreciate this opportunity to connect, share our days, debrief important events, and just hear each other's voice. It is that "last call of the day" many couples look forward to.

While cell phone technology is a wonderful thing, dropped calls and poor signals come along with the territory, so from time to time we get disconnected. When this happens, one of us will call the other back and we resume the conversation. Occasionally it takes a little longer though. I will sometimes call back and it will go straight to voicemail, and I'll have to try again, or vice versa. Or maybe we are both trying each other at the same time so neither of us gets through. There have been times when it has taken considerable effort, but we always do eventually reconnect.

One recent evening we were disconnected and I was unable to get back in touch with her. I tried several times, and rather than it going straight to voicemail, her phone just rang and rang. I waited patiently for her to call me back, but that did not happen either. I texted her and asked her to just let me know if everything was okay, but received no response. Time passed and eventually I grew a little concerned. I knew chances were that everything was probably all right, but that doubt was still gnawing at me. This had never happened before. What if something was wrong?

It was a judgment call whether or not to drive to her house. I could go just to be on the safe side, but I would risk waking her household and causing a disturbance. I could ignore it and go to sleep, but if it turned out something had been wrong I would be kicking myself later. I turned to the inner teacher, my spiritual guide, the Prophet, and asked for guidance. I simply turned my attention more inwardly, stilled my thoughts as much as possible and rose above the situation, asking to see it from a higher perspective. I immediately felt a sense of relief and relaxation come over me, an unmistakable inner knowing that told me everything was okay. I heard Prophet tell me, "There is a perfectly logical explanation for this. Just relax and go to sleep," and go to sleep I did. I trusted the communication and let go of any doubt, falling into a deep and peaceful slumber.

Sometime during the night I was given a dream. In the dream I was looking at my cellphone and saw a text from my girlfriend. It was a text telling me everything was okay and explaining why she had not been able to call back. I then awakened physically from this dream. It was three-thirty in the morning and I felt a nudge to look at my actual cellphone. There was the text from her in the physical – the same text I had just seen in the dream! There was indeed a "perfectly logical explanation" for what had happened, just as Prophet had advised me.

This experience reminded me of the importance of inner knowing, and that it is one of the highest forms of spiritual communication. Having these several data points strengthened my truth detector even more. I am so loved that Spirit also gave me a dream as a confirmation and then a physical text as well! The dream provided much appreciated reinforcement to the inner knowing, and the physical text was just icing on the cake. Human consciousness sometimes gets it backwards; placing the greatest importance on physical communication. Moreover, while the physical is often unreliable and intermittent, communication with God, especially when nurtured, is rock solid.

I am grateful for this experience on many levels. Not to be overlooked is simply my gratitude to have communication with the Divine. God loves us and is there to guide us every day and in every way, from the profound to the seemingly mundane. Having Divine communication helped me in a real-world, everyday situation, giving me practical guidance I could immediately apply. I was able to rely on and trust my inner communication even when my outer communication failed. What a priceless and reassuring gift!

Written by Laurence Elder

32

Flight Lessons for Soul

*In dreams you can experience your true nature, Soul,
an eternal spiritual being. The lessons you learn during
inner travels in the dream worlds can carry into your
waking life, making life in the physical an
even greater joy.*

In this dream I was receiving flying lessons
from an instructor along with a couple other
students. The instructor symbolized my spiritual
teacher, Prophet Del Hall III. I was seated on a
wooden chair bottom and had a cushion
wrapped around my back and under my arms.
There was no plane or other flying apparatus,
engine, wings or anything else you might expect
needed to fly in the physical. I began going up
and down by simply thinking about it and
focusing on where I wanted to go.

In the beginning the scenes that went by were
basic flat landscapes that did not require much
maneuvering. Then the scenes changed abruptly.
I came to a huge drop-off with a massive,

beautiful snow-covered mountain range in front of me. At first I began to back up because it seemed too advanced and it scared me, but soon my instructor (who could communicate with me without talking) said to go ahead – I was ready and I could do this. "Just fly it like I taught you," he said. There was nothing visibly protecting me from falling out of the seat, but I knew that if I just flew as I was taught and did not think of bad things, I would be okay. So I ventured forward, and the depths and expanse opened up - it was awesome! Then it was time to come back to the ground. We were checking out someone's backcountry property on the way down and having fun exploring. I thought it would take a while like landing an airplane, but it was almost immediate, and it was a smooth landing.

Even though I had this dream almost a year ago, it continues to teach and encourage me. This dream experience especially helps me when I am faced with a new or challenging situation or need some reassurance. At those times I hear Prophet's voice saying, "Just fly it like I taught you", and I know he is right there with me. This dream was a real experience, and it is evidence of the true nature of Soul. The inner worlds are an amazing, vast, and adventure-filled place to explore. As Soul, I am not constrained or limited by things of the physical. With Prophet's guidance and instruction I can travel and experience things just by thinking or shifting my focus (consciousness). This, and much more, is part of Soul's boundless nature Prophet can help one experience and more fully manifest in daily life.

Written By Lorraine Fortier

33

I Feel Right With God

Dreams are so much more than simply images. They are not just a television set projected by the mind on the back of our eyelids we passively watch. They are memories of our active experiences in the greater worlds of Spirit and one way that God can teach and bless us. Sometimes a dream might contain a profound truth and leave no visual memory but rather a knowingness. Do not discount these.

It was early March and I could hear the cold biting wind outside nipping at the windows of the log cabin in which we were staying. I was in that cozy place between the dream world and the world where my physical body lay resting. I tried to gently go over my dream so I could record it in my dream journal. Eyes still closed, I continued to stay in that space, savoring it. No images of the recent adventures drifted into my consciousness, just a feeling, and a deep, solid-as-a-rock, sink-your-teeth-into, kind of feeling. I rubbed the sleep from my eyes, pulled my dream journal closer to write, and lay there stumped. I had no words to write. I could not remember any details of the experience I had just left.

Journaling my dreams is one way I demonstrate gratitude for the sacred experiences I have been given, so pulling my pen cap off I began to write. "I don't remember my dream, but I woke up feeling right with God." I climbed down the ladder to the main cabin area and after a warm breakfast of home-cooked oatmeal our small group gathered at the table for class. We began by sharing our dreams from the night before with our teacher Del Hall.

Soon it was my opportunity to share. I felt a little sheepish thinking I did not have much to contribute. Del listened with full attention as I shared not remembering my dream but waking up and feeling right with God. Del's eyes smiled as he said, "One of the most important aspects of a dream is what God is trying to communicate to us." He continued, "Most people would love to wake up feeling right with God." I sat there jaw slightly dropped. "I feel right with God!" The gravity and magnitude of those seemingly simple words sunk in slowly. My heart overflowed with love. I was immediately glad I had spoken up and shared my dream, and even more grateful to Del for personally helping me understand the gift of love I had been given.

To this day I cherish that dream. I often revisit that moment of being snuggled warm in my sleeping bag and nestled in God's Heart. That feeling so lovingly placed in my heart continues to bless me. It provides me with spiritual nourishment, bringing me comfort and strength when the storms in life make the surface waves choppy, and I seek something solid under my feet.

Back in the cabin at the Nature Awareness School, Del's discourse on dreams continued as we learned how to become more fluent in the "Language of the Divine," to better understand the subtle inner communication we all have. Del taught us many things that morning such as: at times all we may remember when we wake is a sound or a color; at other times we wake with just a feeling or a knowing that a personal message from God was placed directly in our hearts. I felt a week's worth of learning and truth was imparted into our hearts in the following hours, and before we could blink it was time for lunch.

Sitting around that table, warmed by the steadily burning fire in the wood stove and the truth in Del's words, I learned the importance of trusting my experiences. I learned the importance of having a teacher to personally help me understand the blessings I have been given. Especially when it is a "simple dream," like waking up feeling right with God.

Written by Ahna Spitale

34

A Dream of Deep Peace

When you know deep down that God loves you it is the ultimate comfort. No matter what comes up in life you can rest assured you are not alone and you will get through it. What joy life can be to live with the deep peace this confidence brings.

It was an ordinary night as my head rested on the pillow, and I took a moment to reflect back on the day. There were so many blessings, all gifts of God in the moments that make up the day. With my heart full of gratitude I began to sing HU, a love song to God, taught to me by Prophet Del Hall III at the Nature Awareness School. At some point I asked for a dream and drifted off to sleep.

When I woke in the morning, I did not have much to write. It was a quick flash. I had just a glimpse of the dream at first, but the feeling of it was solid, tangible, and important. I wrote "A Deep Peace." As I put pen to paper more and more remembrance came. God responded. A prayer was answered to have a dream and He was helping me remember it. I made the effort to do my part asking and writing this sacred communication, and the blessings unfolded. I was reminded of something in my heart – to walk each day in deep peace, and not just feeling or thinking, but knowing I am Soul, loved by God and guided by His Prophet.

I saw myself on the sand beside Prophet in the beauty of an ocean of God's Light and Love. It was peaceful, calm, and quiet with melodic waves. Everything in my vision was blue, as if I were looking through a lens. As the images became clearer, I could see it was because at the same time I was also submerged in that ocean. I sat next to the inner Prophet well below the surface, encompassed in God's Love. We were far down where there is a stillness, peace, and calm. I could see the waves pass above. Some were soft and some crashed hard, much like my life, but where we were it was still. The surface waves existed, but they did not rattle us. I was aware of these waves, but they did not bounce us about. In that moment I was with Prophet - trusting, abiding, connected, and as Soul very thankful to be in the Hands of God. These are the important things. The deep peace in my heart could only be experienced and not described by mere words. It settled into my core, and at the same time I knew it had always been there. I clearly saw this as a gift from God that Prophet was revealing, like was a hidden door. There was strength in this knowing.

Deep in the water I was not gasping for air worried about drowning, but soaking in the moment and surroundings with gratitude. This image and experience is a reference that helps anchor me in peace. Situations arise, but from the perspective of deep in that ocean, as Soul with Prophet, it all looks different. There is a peace and confidence like nothing in this physical world, and I am able to act instead of react to all of those surface waves of life. I go about the responsibilities of my day, but know that I am Soul, God loves me, and there is so much more. A problem does not seem so big. An enjoyable moment is cherished more because I recognize it is fleeting and a gift. I can be in and not of this world when Prophet leads me, stable in that ocean where there is everything we truly need. I choose to walk in that deep peace. Thank you for showing me the way Prophet.

Written by Michelle Hibshman

35

Prophet Provides

Growth is part of life, and experiences that stretch us past our comfort zone provide some of the biggest opportunities to grow. The author of this story is comforted with the realization that no matter what new adventure in life awaits, he has been prepared for it.

My relationship with Prophet of the times is blessing our family. In October of 2014 I attended a retreat at the Nature Awareness School. My wife and I were expecting our first baby in a few weeks. I had a mixture of excitement and also some anxiety about what to expect and how to embark on the grand adventure of fatherhood. I went to bed that night asking Prophet for a dream. I awoke in the middle of the night not recalling a specific dream, but with the baby on my mind. I trusted God would give me all I needed to be a great dad, but I had no idea what that was. I had not had this life experience yet and was not sure how to go about it. I then rolled over and fell back asleep. Fortunately Prophet knows what is in our hearts, and without my asking for it specifically he gave me a dream that offered reassurance and confidence.

In the dream I was given a job in a university laboratory. I was part of a small group of Souls and standing before us were these large space-age looking metal containers that seemed like they were storing something for the future. There was one specifically for each of us. We opened the outer case and inside was a glass vessel full of clear, super-cooled liquid. The fluid was slowly being drained down to expose shelves holding smaller containers of liquid. We each got to look inside and take inventory of our container's contents, but had to wait to open the smaller vessels and discover what was stored within. The container and super-cooled liquid inside had been preserving these gifts, and I had a feeling this cargo vessel came here to Earth between forty and fifty years ago. It was as if this storage vessel contained everything I would ever need for any situation in my life. I awoke with the feeling that with Prophet I was now equipped with everything I needed to work through any situation in my life.

When we gathered the next morning we had the opportunity to share our dreams with the class. While sharing my dream with Del Hall IV and the class, something very special happened. I was given the realization: Hey, I am between forty and fifty years old. Maybe God sent this vessel here with me to help me thrive in whatever experiences may come my way. I had a feeling that when the time came these gifts would be activated, but not until I needed them and the time was right. With Prophet, these things were now available to me. They were always here my whole life waiting for the conditions to be ripe, but I had no idea they even existed. With this realization came a knowing, and with this knowing came a great peace and confidence. Whatever experiences lay before me, I would know what to do, and my actions would be a blessing to my family. I did not need to have all the answers up front; they would come in the proper time.

It makes sense that if God is going to give us an experience he is going to give us the tools to make the most of it. I felt different; I was now filled with a peace and confidence unknown to me before. This gift from God gave me the strength and confidence I needed to grow through the early months of my daughter's life, and it continues today. What a blessing. Why does God give us dreams such as these?

Because we are loved, and dreams are one of the many ways God expresses His Love for His children.

Written by Mark Snodgrass

36

Will You Know It When You Find It?

Eternity abounds in that precious moment when time stands still and a vision from the past becomes the present reality. Knowing you are in the right place and on the right track for your journey home to God is such a reassuring gift of peace and comfort.

I look forward each night to having dreams. My dreams come to me in many forms. Some are vivid, clear, and full of easy to understand details, like watching a movie. Others are jumbled, vague, and don't seem to make much sense. Some mornings I awake with a knowing, a word or phrase, or a feeling that becomes clearer over time, and further thoughts are given to me. Then there are the dreams that really stand out, dreams of a quality more refined, with deep emotions I know are special gift and come for a reason and may take some time before I know the meaning. I would like to share with you such a dream.

While growing up I had a recurring dream that came to me for several years. Each time I experienced this dream it was like being with a childhood friend you know and love. A friend you trust, a friend you have shared experiences with, a friend who knows your hopes and dreams and you know theirs. It was a simple dream of a place I hoped I would someday be taken to.

In the dream I am standing at the base of a group of large boulders that form an outcrop of rocks with spaces between the rocks like small caves. This area is far up on a ridge overlooking a forested valley with another ridge opposite. There is a pole tied between two posts or trees I imagined would be used to tie a horse to. My thought had been that this place was out west somewhere in cowboy country. The sun is bright and warm. The area at my feet appears to have been cleared and used as a sheltered place to spend the night. I don't see myself or anyone else, but I know I am not there alone.

Each time I dreamed of this place it became more real. The feeling was one of belonging and having deep peace. Throughout my younger years it seemed this dream came to me at times when I needed reassurance and comfort. I would awake smiling, knowing all was right with the world. As I grew into my teens, to adulthood, and to retirement, this dream faded in my memory, until...

During my years at the Nature Awareness School I have enjoyed the solo time we are given during classes to explore the property in the Blue Ridge Mountains. The school is a visually and spiritually beautiful part of the world that has been offered to the students to enjoy. While attending my early classes, I heard about a place on the property that was a challenge to get to. It had a carving of a face on a tree done many years ago. No one knew who had done this carving. During some solo time I was drawn to find this place. I climbed down through the rocks in the area I was told it was located and soon found it. When I turned around to leave I was standing in the exact place I had seen in my dreams over fifty years ago. Time stopped. I knew eternity in that moment. The sun was bright and warm, there was the pole to "tie up a horse," the ground and view were as in the dream, and a profound peace filled my being. I knew the presence of the Lord.

I now know that Prophet has been with me, preparing and comforting me, throughout my life to bring me to that moment of realization, that place of the dream he gave me. This is where I belong, a trailhead on my continuing spiritual journey home to the Heart of God. Thank you.

Written by Terry Kisner

Visiting Loved Ones in Dreams

Life on Earth is an interesting venture for sure. It is here we experience the joys and pains of the physical world. Of these, the loss of a loved one is for many the hardest. It matters not if it is a family member, friend, neighbor, or even a pet. Love is love and loss is loss. Even if our faith in God and confidence in Heaven is strong, it still hurts when someone we love is no longer in our immediate reality.

For those not sure about the afterlife or if there even is one, the loss of a loved one can be even more upsetting. What happens to them? Is Heaven real or is it "lights out" forever? Are they okay? Do they remember me? Do they still love me and will I see them again? These questions can rob us of peace and happiness in our daily lives. Imagine how much sweeter it would be to know with confidence your loved ones are alive and well spiritually, and you will see them again. Even better, you can visit them now in dreams.

Although their physical bodies are gone, your loved ones still exist spiritually. The love connection you share is still alive and well. As a gift of love, God and God's Prophet can arrange for you to visit them in a dream. We have been blessed to hear and witness countless examples of the healing that occurs, myself included, when someone has the chance to reconnect with a loved one who has passed on.

What an amazing blessing! How marvelous it is to see a loved one again, to hear their voice, smell their favorite perfume, or to feel their embrace just as real as in the physical. What joy to have an opportunity to look into their eyes and tell them one more time you love them. Even more so if you never had the chance to do this before they passed. These very real experiences are opportunities that will help heal your heart.

The stories in this section are just a few of the examples of the profound blessings gained from reconnecting with loved ones in dreams. If you would like to read more on this subject, another of our books, "Visit Loved Ones in Heaven," contains thirty-seven testimonies of people being reunited with loved ones in dreams, contemplations, and guided Soul travel experiences.

37

My Mother's Love is Always With Me

The love between two Souls does not cease at the end of physical life. It is eternally alive and well. Not only is their love for us present in our daily lives, we can visit them spiritually in dreams and contemplations. What a comfort it is to know these truths through experience.

Each Christmas my mother would save one gift and place it on our dinner plates. I was always so excited to open this extra gift. It was one of the many ways she demonstrated her love for me. As a child I never thought I would lose my mother; I doubt any child ever thinks about losing a parent. I was twenty-one when she passed and it was devastating. I had no air to breathe; no blood to beat my heart. All ceased to exist. I had categorically never felt anything worse than the pain that accompanied losing my mother, and I wasn't sure how to survive. I ached for just one more second with her, one more glimpse of her beautiful smile, one more hug, or to be able to say "I love you" just one more time. I would give anything to have just one more moment with her.

My father taught me from a young age to listen to my dreams for Divine guidance. I am so appreciative and grateful to him for teaching me the ways of God. Recently I was looking through some of my old, really old, dream journals. I came across a dream from 2001, three years after my mother passed. In the dream I was very sad and I was asking my mother to visit me every night. She told me "I am with you every night, I am always with you." I was upset that I could not remember the times when she came to see me, and I asked her to please help me remember these visits together. I knew when I saw her in my dreams that she was indeed with me, and I longed to be conscious of our precious moments together.

During a HU Sing at the Nature Awareness School fourteen years later, I was blessed by Prophet to be united again with my mother. She looked so beautiful and joyful. The happiness I felt when I saw her is indescribable; I was overcome with joy and love. She told me again "I am with you every night, I am always with you." I was transported back to my dream experience from all those years ago, and I knew that she has always been with me and will always be with me. She is not with me physically, but a part of her is always with me. Her love is forever with me.

I cherish every time I am blessed by God to have another moment with my mother. I know these are real experiences and we are visiting with each other as Soul. These visits with her helped heal my heart, and I believe heal her heart as well. Our love for each other endures, not bound by physical limitations. Like the gifts on my Christmas dinner plate, these extra moments with my mother are special gifts from God because of His deep Love for me. I thank my father for teaching me the ways of God as a child; I thank God and Prophet for blessing me with these treasured moments with my mother.

Written by Emily Allred

38

Dad Helped Me From Heaven

Dads can shower their children with love in many ways. It may come as a smile or pat on the back, words of encouragement or wisdom, quality time together, or in the following example a reminder to check the oil in the lawn mower. The fact that the reminder came in a dream after the author's father had passed demonstrates how this love transcends physical life.

Growing up I loved my dad dearly. He was loving, gracious, and had a good nature. He taught my brother and me many outdoor sports such as skiing, ice-skating, canoeing, sailing, archery, and shooting at cans with his .22 rifle. We spent many hours enjoying the outdoors with him and my mom, camping and doing many of those things he taught us. As a teenager I would help him in his carpentry business by painting and staining wood trim. I enjoyed hanging out with him in his workshop while I helped him with projects, and we talked about all sorts of things. After my brother went off to college we bought season passes at a ski slope nearby. We spent many hours skiing together. I was his precious little girl and I always knew that he loved me. I thought that he would always be there for me.

I was seventeen years old when my dad was diagnosed with an inoperable brain tumor. The doctor told us that with radiation treatments he might live for another five years. Back in the 1970s no one talked with the patient about how serious their condition was or that they might die, but somehow he knew. Because we didn't talk about it, we never got a chance to say goodbye. Two months after the diagnosis, even with the treatments, he was in the hospital dying, unable to communicate with us. During his time in the hospital he visited me in a dream. He was going up and down in an elevator. I saw him, though we did not speak. Somehow I knew it was real and we were really together.

A few days after he died I planned to mow the lawn. He had given me a nice new bright yellow lawn mower about a year before, after the old one quit working. He even put on a miniature license plate with my name on it. A loving touch. That night I had a very clear dream. He came to remind me to check the oil in the lawnmower. The next day before starting up the mower I remembered the dream so I checked the oil. The oil compartment was bone dry! Thanks Dad for your help in a dream! Back then I didn't know whom to thank for giving me the dream, but I was grateful for it.

Over twenty years later, after getting married and having two children, I began going to the Nature Awareness School with my husband. I learned about the Prophet of the times and that one way he blesses us is with dreams. One night I had a dream where I was told I was now allowed to see my father. He appeared before me and I could see his facial features very clearly. He looked strong and healthy, like he was before he got sick. We hugged and hugged for a long time. He felt so real and so solid. It was so good to see him, to hug him, and to feel his love again. I felt such intense joy seeing him. I said it had been twenty-two years since I last saw him. Gosh, twenty-two years! When we stopped hugging, he disappeared. What a gift that was! It was real. We were two Souls seeing each other again after almost twenty-two years. Thank you, Prophet!

Now, for the rest of the story. Several years after that dream I learned, through many awake dreams and a knowingness, that he had reincarnated into another body as someone with whom I have a very close relationship. God has blessed us with being together again. Our love continues, beyond death and into life again!

Written by Diane Kempf

39

Dreams Have Kept Our Relationship Alive

*Even though our time in the physical comes to an end,
we will see our loved ones again. Until then, dreams
afford us with a very real opportunity to continue our
relationship by spending time together. The love we
experience in dreams is just as real as in waking life.*

My grandmother passed away when I was a
young child. At the time I was confused about
her death. It was the first time I can remember
experiencing the feeling of loss and deep
sadness. We were very close and I loved her very
much. Sometime shortly after her death,
however, I had a dream with her. In the dream
we spent time together in her workshop. She
used to make beautiful stained glass artwork and
windows. I sat on her workbench and watched
her make stained-glass windows enjoying our
time together. I do not recall our talking in the
dream, but I experienced the bond of love we

shared. This dream brought me a lot of comfort during a time of hurt. My heart began to heal from the loss and over the years I would have a dream with her from time to time.

I had dreams where she was at some of my sports games cheering me on. I saw her seated in the bleachers smiling and happy. These dreams were so real that when I would wake up a part of me knew she was not gone forever and was fine wherever she was. At the age of twenty I moved from a small town in Colorado to the Northern Virginia area. This was a big transition for me. Shortly after my move I had another dream with my grandma where she looked at me and into my eyes and said, "It's all alright." I awoke from that dream with a feeling of comfort and peace that I cherished during a time where everything around me was new and unfamiliar. My dreams had become a way for our relationship to continue even though she had passed on.

A few years after my move, I began taking classes at the Nature Awareness School. There I learned that dreams are a way the Divine communicates with us, and each of us has our own personal dream language. This resonated with me, and my dream experiences over the years with my grandmother only confirmed this truth. The school helped me really claim that these are REAL experiences. This realization has been a beautiful blessing in my life, and it has shown me that our loved ones live on beyond the physical. The dreams with my grandma over the years have brought me comfort, love, peace, and helped heal the hurt I experienced in her passing.

Our dreams are REAL experiences. We may not always understand them and sometimes they may seem convoluted. But I can truly say I understand more of my personal dream language through the spiritual tools I have learned at the Nature Awareness School.

Written by Shanna Canine

40

Closure With Grandmother

We live in a temporal world where everything has a beginning and an end. Soul however is eternal and carries on after its time in the physical world; it does not cease. In the dream state you can visit with loved ones who have gone on before you. These encounters are not simply wishful thinking on the mind's part; they are real experiences and a profound blessing.

One night I had a dream with my grandmother. She had passed away some time ago, and I had never been able to have that last conversation with her. I only got to say a quick goodbye on the phone the night she passed.

In this dream we got to spend some time together and have that conversation. I was getting out of a vehicle in a restaurant parking lot and was looking around. This place was not familiar to me. I saw someone waving at me from the front door. It was my grandmother! She looked much younger than her years. She was smiling and waving me over. I ran to her and gave her a big hug. We walked in, sat down, and began to talk. We talked about all of the things that I had wanted to tell her before she passed. I had a chance to tell her how much I loved and missed her, and I thanked her for all she did for me in life.

I felt like the Divine set this up for the both of us. We both had things we felt we needed to tell the other, and through the Grace of God we had the chance to do so. I am so grateful to the Divine for allowing me the opportunity to spend that time with her. It meant so much to me to tell her, face to face, one last time that I love her.

Written by Anthony Allred

41

Grateful for the Time I Had

*This story is about more than the loss of a beloved pet.
It is about having the wisdom, trust, and strength to
focus on the positive in a time of genuine sadness.
Those who have this attitude of gratitude will be able
to travel through the rough patches in life with less
wear and tear.*

I am eleven years old and I had an amazing, amiable boy cat named Adam. His personality was adorable and I loved him dearly. He knew how to give and receive love. On March 11, 2015 my family and I had to take him to the veterinarian and put him down. He had a urinary tract infection which had damaged his kidneys. He was only three years old and I was extremely sad! I trusted God and knew in my heart this happened for a reason, but it still hurt. Even so, I decided it would be better to be grateful for the time I had with him instead of being sad about the time I didn't.

I know you can visit loved ones in dreams so I asked Prophet several times over the next few nights for a dream with Adam. I did not receive one right away but kept asking and never gave up. One night I had a wonderful dream with him, it was so clear. In the dream I was climbing the stairs to my room to go to sleep. When I opened the door Adam was sitting right there on the floor next to my bed. Once Adam saw me he quickly scrambled under the bed like some cats do. Sadly I got in bed, wishing he had not scurried away. He then peaked his head out with a look on his face that said, "Oh… you want to pet me." He then snuggled up close to me purring loudly. I could feel his warmth as I scratched his furry little head. It felt so real! I cried both joyful and sad tears. I am very grateful that God and Prophet knew I missed him. It helped me a lot seeing him again.

After a few months I started wondering about getting another kitten as a gift for my upcoming birthday. I then received a magazine I subscribe to and it had a kitten on the cover, which it never does. The month of the issue was my birthday month. I was then reading a book and the girl who had always wished for a kitten received one for her birthday. I took these signs as confirmation of what was in my heart: I was ready for and desired another cat.

I will always have a strong love for Adam as well as for my new kitten, Milo. I'll always remember Adam and the amazing gift that God gave me.

Written by Zoe Hall

42

River of Life

It is always special to see a loved one in a dream. When you visit a loved one who has already passed it is a very special blessing. These experiences can bring closure, peace, and joy! These are real experiences, not just wishful thinking on the part of your mind. The following is a beautiful example of this.

When I grew up I had a favorite uncle, Uncle Ed. A few years ago he was unexpectedly diagnosed with a life-threatening illness. He was healthy and relatively young, so this news took the whole family by surprise. Uncle Ed's health failed rapidly and within a year he was in hospice. Soon after entering hospice he passed away.

A little while after he passed, I was given the following dream. Uncle Ed, his wife Roslyn, and I were kayaking down the most beautiful river on a warm spring day. The water flowed gently, a breeze cooled our skin, and beautiful foliage dipped into the water's surface. The three of us enjoyed this day together, laughing and taking in the scenery.

We were each in our own kayak. At times we were close together and at other times we were farther apart as we floated down the beautiful river. I awoke with a feeling of joy and peace, grateful to have seen my uncle again. I know it was really him, and we got to spend one more day together.

I know it was a Divine gift to see my uncle again, but there was even more to the dream. For me this dream carried another spiritual message. The river represented the "River of Life." Sometimes we were close together on the river. This represented the lifetimes when we were both incarnated and able to talk on the phone or be together physically. At other times in the dream we were farther apart on the river. This represented the current time, when he had passed away and we were no longer able to be together physically. This dream showed me that even when we are farther apart on the "River of Life," he is fine. He is in another realm, but he is healthy, lively, and loved. I still miss him, but it is good to know he is happy and enjoying his new life in one of the worlds of God.

This dream reinforced for me that our loved ones do carry on after they pass, and that our love connection with them transcends our physical connection. I am grateful for the teachings I have received from Del which made it possible for me to recognize and accept the Divine blessing of this dream.

Written by David Hughes

43

My Answered Prayer

*You are an eternal spiritual being whose lessons,
growth, and journey will continue on after the end of
this physical life. Whether you are here on Earth or in
one of the numerous inner worlds (Heavens), there is
always more wisdom and love to be gained.*

My dad passed away almost ten years ago,
although it seems like only yesterday. Even
though time has passed I still think of my dad
often, and recently became aware of a prayer in
my heart to know he was okay.

Prophet of God blessed me one night with a
dream in answer to my heart's prayer. This
incredible, vivid dream showed me that not only
was my dad okay, but he was learning and
growing spiritually as Soul even after the death
of his physical body.

The dream took place in the house my dad
built, the house where I grew up. In the dream I
walk slowly up the front driveway. I am aware of
the meticulously landscaped front lawn. I peer

through a window of a previously unfinished room that had been my dad's workshop. Lights are on inside and the room is now completely finished and decorated. Bookshelves with books neatly arranged line the walls. A brightly burning lamp sits next to a recliner chair with someone, I'm thinking my dad, relaxing and reading in it.

Continuing on, I follow the driveway and proceed to the back of the house. A sign posted on the newly mowed lawn announces the place is available to rent for family picnics and gatherings. I open the kitchen door and call inside, "Is anyone home?" A grey-haired man, trim and very friendly, greets me and asks why I am here. I explain that my dad built this house. Smiling, he then leads me on a tour of the house telling me how wonderful a job my dad has done in completing and remodeling it.

Upon awakening I immediately wrote down this vivid and detailed dream in my dream journal, and asked Prophet for guidance in interpreting it. Prophet lovingly showed me this house represents my dad's spiritual house. It has been remodeled; he is growing spiritually. Rooms in this house that were incomplete are now complete and brightly lit with God's Love. The rental of the back yard for family picnics and gatherings represents my dad's growth in the area of being more open and welcoming with family and others. Love is growing and flourishing here.

This beautiful gift of love from Prophet was an answer to my heart's prayer.

We are Soul, and as Soul we are eternal; God's Prophet is with us always as we continue to grow and learn even after the death of our physical body. How blessed we are!

Written by Donna Hospodar

Past-Life and Prophetic Dreams

When viewed from the perspective of Soul you have a single lifetime to live. Soul is eternal; it lives forever. However, Soul incarnates many many times within a new physical body to continue Its journey of learning more about giving and receiving love. Along the way Soul picks up likes and dislikes from Its vast number of experiences. Consciously we may not remember our previous lives, but they have helped shape who we are today. If it is in our best spiritual interest Prophet will reveal a past life to us in a dream. Prophet may also use a dream to shed light on a future event. In both cases it is done to help us in our current life.

44

My Dream Foresaw Change Coming

In most cases dreams are about the dreamer's life, versus the world in general. Dreams involving major earth changes, natural disasters, world events, and the like usually point to personal changes.

I had a dream in early 2004 which taught me through personal experience some valuable lessons, that Prophet and his son Del Hall IV had been teaching me about for years. When I came across the dream years later, I realized the prophetic dream had come true, but not in the way I initially interpreted.

The dream was simple. I was on a hillside watching lots of changes happening on a worldwide scale. People were reacting to the change in different ways: some were fearful, some stressed, some relaxed. I knew in the dream I was being shown the future, the year 2006. A year of worldwide change. When I awoke, I wrote down the dream. I took it literally, thinking there may be catastrophic change coming. Trusting the dream information was accurate, and liking to be prepared, I ordered some extra rice and beans to store in my basement, but mostly forgot about the dream during my day-to-day life.

Two years later I came across the journal that contained this simple dream. I was unpacking books and journals onto shelves in the new house my husband and I had just bought together. We had recently moved to a new town across the mountain from where I had spent most of my childhood, and I was joyfully pregnant with our first child, due to arrive in a few months. It was December 2006. Great change had just occurred in my world. A new marriage, a new house, a new town, and a new pregnancy all in the year 2006! It truly had been a prophetic dream. God knew what was coming in my life.

Our dreams can have several layers of meaning which relate to different aspects of our lives. They are given to bless us and are usually about us and our lives, but sometimes our initial interpretation is not accurate. It is important to stay open to more information. If God has something important to communicate to us, He will continue to express it until we get it, provided we are receptive. By staying open I received the accurate meaning of the dream.

God still sends, through His Prophet, prophetic dreams to guide, provide counsel, protect, or give hope for the future to His children! His help in dreams is not just reserved for saints in the Bible, but is available for all of His children. God is a living God and He truly loves us. One way God can bless us is through our dreams. In this dream I received a message from Him about my personal life. It is possible for you too!

I had not recognized it at the time, but as my life was about to change all around me, it had been foreseen. God knew before it even happened. What comfort that brought me as I sat on the floor unpacking. It still brings me comfort today. My life was foreseen, as is yours. God knows. We are not alone.

Written by Molly Comfort

45

Dream With Past-Life Records

It is true that you only live one life, but not in the sense that most people have been taught. You are Soul, an eternal spiritual being. You do not "have" a soul, you are Soul. You are one Soul, the same Soul, for all eternity. However, Soul lives many different physical lifetimes. Each serves as a unique opportunity to grow in wisdom and love.

During a morning contemplation I asked Prophet for some insight about a relationship in my life. Afterwards I went about my day. Just before bed I thought about the things and people in my life I am very grateful for, then I drifted off to sleep.

I joined Prophet in a dream. We walked through a beautiful garden courtyard, entered a set of glass doors, and walked down a hallway into a very plain and simple room. After we sat and talked for a little while some people came in to visit with me. Most of the people I knew from the past. Some of them were very good friends, a few of them I had not seen in years, and others looked familiar, but I could not recall from where I knew them. This caught my attention and raised some questions. Where was I and what was going on? Was it my birthday or had I died?

Prophet brought me back from my thoughts. He directed my attention from the people in the room to a nearby wall covered in a very beautiful and unusual wallpaper. It was made up of hundreds or thousands of tiny photos, images, or scenes. At a glance this made up a bigger picture. I was surprised when I noticed that the larger picture was an image of me. As a visual reference for the reader, a few weeks after this dream I came across an image made in a very similar way called a photo mosaic. The image in my dream appeared to be alive and fluid. Though the majority of the images were unfamiliar, as I looked more closely I saw a few of them were from significant periods in my present life.

Prophet explained to me this giant collage was a record of many of my past lives, with hundreds and thousands of little images and scenes from hundreds and thousands of years. As he talked he slowly walked down the hall, I followed. He turned, stopped, and faced the wall. There I noticed a small image that for some reason brought a smile to my face. In this picture there was an eighth century Chinese warrior riding a beautiful gray horse across rolling green hills. I knew it was me from a long time ago. I remembered that day, my horse, and that particular valley. In the picture next to it I saw myself walking in the hot desert during the time period when various pyramids were being built.

As I looked around I saw many other scenes and though the person I saw in them did not look the way I do now, I clearly knew each had been me. The settings or surroundings I saw myself in varied widely. At times I had been in ancient forests or on white sandy beaches, at others inside castles or next to primitive huts. In other pictures I was in what appeared to be long-forgotten cities or among civilizations that no longer existed.

Prophet chuckled, and I looked over to see what he was looking at. "Here I am," he said pointing to a person in one of the scenes. "What were you doing," I asked? He said, "Watching you, cheering you on!" He smiled. As he did he gazed into my eyes and I felt an incredible wave of love wash through me. I remembered this ancient love from many other lives deep in my heart. He showed me many such lifetimes, picture after picture where he, the Prophet, was watching over me, guiding me, and indeed cheering me on. In most of the lifetimes I had not been aware of the Prophet's presence, though in some of them I was blessed to be aware of and have a conscious relationship with him.

When I looked back at the pictures again, many of the images were moving and playing out a scene from a specific time. Prophet took his hand and touched one of the pictures. As he did it zoomed forward and the picture became life-sized and alive. We walked inside this living scene. For that moment, while I was in the scene, I had no recall of being in the hallway looking at pictures or of sleeping in my warm bed. I was fully immersed in the experience of that life. I could see, smell, feel, and experience every detail of that time period as clearly as if I was living in it in the present moment. When I had remembered that life, the lesson, and the love, we stepped back out into the hallway with a smooth, flawless transition. I looked at many different images. Prophet offered to take me back into any of the lives I was drawn to or had questions about. This trip back through my personal ancient history was incredible and "off the chart" amazing!

I came back with a new sense of peace and appreciation for the lives we live and how our relationships with others span across eons from one time period to the next. Though our bodies may change in appearance, the relationships and strong bonds of love we form continue on with us from one life to another. I saw many people I knew then and could identify as the same Souls now, even though they looked different physically. In some of the lives I was a white person, in some a black person, in some Chinese, in some male and in some female. The color, sex, or nationality I had been seemed trivial and irrelevant in the big picture. The variations and combinations of race, gender, and nationality are endless but each life is specifically designed to help us experience and learn from a new perspective.

I saw that in different lifetimes I would reincarnate with many of the same Souls. Sometimes we had good relationships and sometimes we rubbed each other like coarse sandpaper, but each life had a common thread which was to teach us all how to give and receive love. Sometimes we were friends, sometimes not, sometimes work associates, other times warriors in combat. The list was endless: farm workers, family members, children or parents, husbands or wives. I thank Prophet for this incredible gift. It provided me with a much clearer understanding of how we are connected, and it helped me have a greater love and appreciation for all the unique Souls and relationships I am blessed by God to have in my life. Through this gift of a dream Prophet also allowed me to see how each person and each life encouraged growth in many different areas. I awoke back in my warm bed.

Later I found out Prophet had taken me to the Causal plane to a temple of learning called Sakapori located in the spiritual city of Honu. The images and lifetimes I saw were kept in what is known as the Akashic records. Shamus-i-Tabriz, the Guardian of the temple and keeper of these records had invited us into this particular temple.

The way Prophet can show us our past lives is as varied and individual as each person. I have seen some of my past lives as files in a file cabinet, have been shown them in dreams, in contemplations, in the beam of light at a spiritual temple, and had glimpses or flashes of them in the course of a normal day. One of the main reasons to be shown past lives is to help us live a better, more fulfilling, joyful, and abundant life this time. Another reason is to help us realize we are Soul, an eternal spark of God, and the real us does not die when our current bodies wear out. A third, and perhaps the most important reason, is to help us know each Soul, whether consciously aware of it or not, has had a long and personal relationship with God and His Prophets through many lifetimes. When we come to the point where we are able to consciously recognize God's Love for us, and then our love for God, we and our lives become greatly blessed.

From this dream and other experiences I have realized past lives are as real as any day in this present life. We have good days and tough days, but we each do the best we can. Each day, like each life, we live, love, grow, and learn a little more. It takes thousands of days in thousands of lifetimes to experience and learn about all the wonderful things God has in store for us and to receive all the gifts and blessings God wants to give us. We exist because God loves us. The lives in which we grow the most are the ones in which we are blessed to have a conscious relationship with and learn from a true Prophet of God. Our potential rate of growth in these lifetimes is exponential. With Prophet's help, guidance, and love we can see the world and

God more clearly, as it truly is, and come to know our Heavenly Father more intimately. This provides a life that is abundant beyond imagination.

Whether we are aware of it or not, God and His Prophet are always with us; guiding, loving, nudging, rooting for, and cheering us on during our journey home to our Heavenly Father.

Written by Jason Levinson

46

Greater Abundance Follows Past-Life Healing

Whether we are conscious of them or not, things from our past effect us in the present. We can attempt to "wall off" or ignore old areas we do not wish to look at, but this does not mean they are gone. When we are ready to face them Prophet can help us disentangle from things that are no longer serving us.

I had a dream I was in my house. It was multi-storied, bright, sunny, and had open space. Suddenly I found myself in a different part of the house I did not know existed, or I had not been in for a long while and had forgotten about. It was on a lower level, perhaps a first floor or basement. It was a separate structure but was attached to my house and shared a common wall. I briefly caught a glimpse of this from the exterior, then was back inside. This attached section was old and in very bad shape.

On my first walk around this attached structure with its large rooms it looked as if they might have potential. I thought maybe I could fix this up and rent it out. Then I looked up and saw the ceilings were near collapsing. I noticed the floors were torn up and debris was everywhere. It looked as if no one had lived there for a while, with just a few remnants of former life there. It was so bad all I could think was how expensive it was going to be to fix all this. It would probably require a home equity loan, which I did not really want to get. It needed to be dealt with right away though, because it was a hazard. I was even afraid of being in there because it was so unsafe. I was also concerned about the way it was attached onto the nice well built home I lived in. I did not want this old section to cause it to collapse or become structurally damaged.

Then something very cool happened. I woke up while still in the dream and became conscious. This has only happened to me once or twice before that I can recall. At first I was relieved I was in a dream and not in any immediate danger. Then, since I was not in my physical body and therefore not constrained by the body's physical limitations, I started trying things I may not have done otherwise, like putting my fists through the wall and jumping up high enough to go through the ceiling and punch into it. I was covered in dust and plasterboard, but knowing it would not collapse on me physically gave me a sense of freedom and boldness to try such things. I realized this dilapidated structure was beyond repair and had to be demolished, and think this was my way of getting things started. I was very concerned when I awoke however, because houses sometimes represent one's state of consciousness when they show up in dreams. Prophet was trying to get my attention to help me, so I asked him for help in understanding the dream he blessed me with.

After a few contemplations and looking at it from different perspectives, he helped me see some pearls contained in the dream. I was excessively attached to something from the past, and it was negatively impacting this life. Perhaps this was not in an overt or easily noticeable way, but in a fundamental or structural way. This was symbolized by the section of house I had not been in for a long time. The sunlit, multi-storied part of the home I usually lived in was positive, but this older attached section was bad off and potentially hazardous. The common wall between the older and newer section suggested that it was something I had a hard time letting go of, there was also an attempt to keep it compartmentalized and isolated or unacknowledged. Even so it was hurting my spiritual growth. I was limiting the freedom, joy, and abundance in my present life by closing my heart or trying to "wall off" this section.

This information was not totally new to me, as months prior to this Prophet had taken me back to a lifetime in the past that was probably the root of the issue. This Soul travel experience was part of a long healing process that continued with this dream. While it is true that just one meeting with God's Prophet can dramatically change one's life for the better, something this delicate and complex in nature cannot be done all at once, not because he is not able to do it, but because it would be too much for someone to try and overcome all at once. In Prophet's perfect loving way, he was gently raising and expanding my awareness of the situation, little by little, at a rate I could handle without being too much or putting me out of balance. All the while I was being held, loved, and protected in the Hand of God, which I was very aware of throughout.

What was significant about this dream was how clearly I saw the situation and understood. The dream spoke to me as Soul in my native language more directly and clearly than any words or mental dialogue could have conveyed to me while awake. What was also very significant was that I woke up in the dream, and with the boldness and confidence of Soul, I began to take an active part in bringing down the old structure. It was a turning point in both understanding and acceptance of truth given to me by Prophet. I was ready to acknowledge it for what it was, let go of what was holding me back, and move forward.

I was driving to work one morning, a little while after this dream occurred, and saw a truck with the words "Precision Remodelers" written on the back. This awake dream caught my attention and I knew it was a message for me. It reminded me of the house dream and how I was concerned in the dream about how to get rid of the old rundown structure without damaging the nice part of the house. I could certainly use a "precision remodeler." I perceived a blessing and inner healing was taking place. Through this entire process that began months earlier with the initial Soul travel experience, and even before then by conditioning and preparing me, Prophet's precision and expertise were helping me dismantle the wall in my heart and attachments to the past without doing damage. He has made it so the love and cherished memories from that time could flow forward into the present without any of the negative baggage, for that has been let go and replaced with Divine Love.

I feel I am being remodeled and upgraded in that I can feel and appreciate love in new and deeper ways. I notice it in a more honest, loving relationship with Prophet, deeper trust, and more precise inner communication with him. I notice it in more genuine and intimate connections and exchanges with friends and family. I have also noticed more Soul-to-Soul interactions with others I meet throughout the day. I even notice it in a deeper savoring, wonder, and appreciation for nature, and in those special little moments when I experience God's Love through the world around me. It is difficult to put into words, but it feels as if a shadow I did not even know I had, cast itself over my already blessed and abundant life, has been removed. I am beginning to see richness, color, and depth of life and love I have not experienced before.

Prophet wants only the best for us and does not want us to settle for anything less than our true potential, and he knows what this is even if we do not. What was already a very nice house, a beautiful life filled with blessings upon blessings, is becoming even more beautiful, more joyful, more love-filled, and more abundant. It is sometimes hard to imagine, but there truly is always more. Anything is possible with Prophet, and with genuine love and rock-solid trust in him our growth, splendor, and potential to be a blessing to others have no limits.

Written by Lorraine Fortier

47

More Freedom Less Worry

*When we are overly attached to the decisions our loved
ones make it becomes harder to love them purely.
They are a child of God first and as such they will never
be on their own. Learning to love them in a relaxed,
peaceful way will help you savor the love connection.*

It came as an unexpected surprise when my
adult daughter decided to attend a HU Sing
during her impromptu visit with us one weekend.
Two weeks prior, before any of us were aware
she'd be visiting, Prophet (my spiritual teacher
and inner guide) appeared to me in what I can
now say was a prophetic dream. In this dream he
explained that my daughter had contacted him
about an upcoming class, indicating in some way
that she wanted to surprise me. It wasn't long
before she did! Two weeks later we were seated
together at a HU Sing hosted by the Nature
Awareness School.

I feel fortunate to have been among those in
attendance that day. Sharing the experience with

my daughter made it that much more special. The moment I closed my eyes and began singing HU, I saw her as a baby securely cradled in the arms of the Divine. I recognized her as Soul, a beautiful glowing bundle of spiritual light and sound. My heart overflowed with an overwhelming sense of gratitude. Different moments from her life began to play out after that, allowing me to experience each one from the perspective of knowing the Presence of God has always been with her and always will be. A higher truth was evident, although she is my daughter in this lifetime; she belongs to God and has always been in the loving arms of her Heavenly Father. The peace and trust I felt in this moment can hardly be put into words. Being totally in the moment, aware of the Presence of God, I experienced detachment from worldly concerns of every kind. Divine love filled my heart and I felt free, free to simply love.

Prophet took me on a personal journey into the higher worlds and it changed me. The experience was tailor-made to bring me peace, trust, and a greater understanding of love, as it is in Heaven. Through this experience I was able to recognize my two grown children as adults, which has positively affected how I interact with them. I am less emotionally attached to their decisions and free from the expectations I once carried of being invited to weigh in on their decisions. I now have room to enjoy their presence and relate to them as treasured friends; precious Souls I am blessed to share this life with as we each make our way home to God.

It is a profound gift to savor the experiences of life together, unfettered by the emotional entanglements I once mistook for love. I am grateful to Prophet for showing me a higher, purer way to love; one that allows me to care in a relaxed and peaceful way.

Written by Sandra Lane

48

Love and Confidence in My Marriage

A marriage founded on love is a sacred thing. This is true for your physical marriage and even your marriage with God. The two work together and both can thrive when based on love, more specifically the expression of love. What good is love if it is not demonstrated?

I was standing in the middle of a huge room in a house that belonged to my husband Mark and me. I knew it was ours, but it was as if I was discovering it for the first time. In front of me was a grand spiral staircase wide enough for three or four people to walk up side by side. Soft sunlight cascaded in from the home's many windows.

I was happy as I walked through seeing the potential that was there. The house was old but sturdy and in good condition. It was like a historic estate with nice details and lots of wood. My perspective changed to the ceiling where I saw a slimy residue built up. It needed some work, but it was worth restoring. When it was done it would be gorgeous. My friends and family were all gathered inside helping Mark and me renovate the house

Later, as I was exploring, I discovered another wing. Two wooden French doors with glass inserts held back a new space. The room was lit with the glow of afternoon sunlight. Peering through the dusty glass I was delighted to see a baby grand piano inside. Excitement coursed through me as I thought of how beautiful this would be when it was finished. This section, I knew, was for the future. It was something we would open up down the road.

I awoke from this dream experience with a light, expansive feeling that filled my being. I knew the house represented my marriage to Mark. At this time we were just past a year of marriage. Our first year had been rocky at times. I was rough around the edges, emotional, and started a lot of fights. Things were getting better, but I still doubted myself. There were moments when I wondered if Mark would decide he had made a mistake.

This dream gave me reassurance. While our marriage in this life was new, the love between us was not. Like this old estate, our relationship was enduring. It had and would continue to weather many seasons. Knowing that Mark and I were again, after lifetimes, restoring and growing in our love, brought me strength. The home had some dirt and residue from the past, but it was just on the surface. Our marriage, like the estate, has a solid foundation. This helped me relax. It showed me we were in a period of transition. Disagreements would come and this was okay!

Peace and gratitude filled my being. I understood that God, via Prophet was healing me through this dream. The experience filled my heart with love and began to push out the doubts and guilt I had created in the past. I had a renewed confidence that all would be well. The sunlight in the home was the Love of God. This love had brought Mark and I together again. God's Love would hold us together and sustain us forever. I also saw how much love and support we had from our friends and family.

Like a living pearl, reflection upon this dream has revealed deeper layers that to this day continue to bring reassurance and peace to my heart. Del, the Prophet, helped me understand this dream has many meanings. The estate, while representing my earthy marriage was also a representation of my spiritual marriage to the Holy Spirit. Both of these marriages are sacred to God.   Written by Carmen Snodgrass

49

Meeting My Husband in a Dream

Often we are given the "eyes to see" at the perfect time in our journey through life. There is no sense in losing sleep just because we did not recognize it earlier. Trust that God's timing is perfect and He knows when we are ready to accept the blessing He has to offer.

Have you ever had the experience where more is shared and understood by looking someone in the eye than by any words exchanged? I was given a dream in which I do not recall any words being spoken, but what was said through a glance altered my life more than any other dream I have had. During a dream over ten years ago, my teacher, the Prophet, introduced me to my future husband. While I had known Chris as a fellow student at the Nature Awareness School for almost five years, our conversations had remained casual, nothing more. We both had been in prior relationships and had not seen more than a friendship and a common love of the school between us. In the late fall of 2004 this began to change, but it was not until a winter night's dream in early 2005 that I was given the eyes to see what could be.

In the dream Prophet was standing before me looking at me with so much love. He knows me so well, has known me forever, wants what was best for me, and to see me truly happy. With love in his eyes Prophet stepped to the side and gave me the eyes to see who stood beside him. Chris stood there with love in his eyes. At this silent introduction Prophet brought us together in this life. I knew in that unspoken moment we had loved each other many times before. What was shared without any words was, "Here is someone who you love and someone who loves you dearly too."

Shortly after the dream Chris and I went on our first date. This dream has become part of our history, now ten years and three beautiful children later. However, our story did not begin with my dream it began many lifetimes ago. For me the dream gave me a remembrance of what once was and a prophecy of what could be, all in the eyes of Prophet and my future husband. While I did not decide to marry him based on this one dream, it was definitely the threshold that opened my eyes to recognize him as the man I love. It was an opportunity to grow in our love for God by learning to express Divine love with each other once again.

As eternal beings the love connection we share with our loved ones spans beyond space and time. The love that builds and grows in one life leads to the next and creates bonds of love that transcend beyond the confines of the physical world. The Divine reconnects us with those we love as a gift of love. We are given opportunities to heal past hurts and celebrate the joy of life together.

It is by the Grace of God that I was given this opportunity to be with my beloved Chris. Thank you Prophet for knowing me so well, and for introducing me in a dream to the man whom I have loved so many times before, and whom I dearly love now. It is a gift that has made me truly happy.

Written by Molly Comfort

Experiences With the Light of God

The focus of this section is to share actual experiences my students have had with God's Light or Sound in a dream. God's Light and Sound are both aspects of the Voice of God and are similar in that they are both vibrations. Generally one experiences the Light of God first and later, after more training, the Sound of God. The Light or Sound of God, which is the Holy Spirit, comes in many forms and can be consciously perceived by inner nudges, knowingness, feelings of peace, clarity, dreams, and spiritual light or sound.

Having conscious experiences with God's Light is vital for any serious student of God's teachings. Many blessings are received when in the presence of God's Light. God's Light contains love that manifests in a multitude of different forms. This love can manifest as peace, joy, clarity, healings, spiritual truth, increased trust in the Prophet's Divine authority, and more.

This is why God has always given His true Prophet, throughout all of history, the authority to share the Light of God with others. These gifts of love are delivered in the perfect dose for each individual. In the beginning the light and love is subtle, almost unrecognizable. However, once the individual is spiritually strengthened, the intensity and receptiveness of the blessings increase greatly.

As God's Prophet, I take great care not to overwhelm a new seeker with too much light and love during the first few retreats at the school. Too much light given too quickly can cause a new seeker to lose balance, unintentionally slowing their spiritual growth. I listen to and precisely follow God's will for each individual. I hope you can gather from these testimonies how exciting it is to witness God's Light. As the Prophet it is such a joy to see the beautiful transformation the Light of God creates in an individual.

Prophet Del Hall III

50

Sweet Dreams

*Singing HU and asking for a dream before falling
asleep helps you tune in and raise up to receive and
better remember the experience. Most importantly it is
also a form of drawing nigh. Anyone seeking a closer
relationship with the Divine should consider this sacred
principle. When you draw nigh to God,
God will respond.*

"Sweet Dreams" with a smiley face was written on the white board by Del, my spiritual teacher at the Nature Awareness School in Love, Virginia. It was one of the first classes I had attended back in the 1990s. When I arrived that day I looked at the grassy dam that held back the waters from the pond and was excited to place my one-person backpacking tent as close to the water as possible.

As I crawled into my tent and made efforts to get comfortable in my sleeping bag I listened to the night sounds of bullfrogs, birds, and insects. The air seemed alive with sound. I was very excited and asked Divine Spirit to please bring me a dream that was in my best spiritual interest and to help me remember it. Del had made those suggestions during class with the option to share our dream experiences in class the next morning.

I sang HU, a pure prayer to God. In a moment I was aware of three spiritual beings kneeling on either side of me. They were made of white translucent light. Silently they wrapped me in what felt like a very soft, deep, downy comforter. The thin sleeping mat on which I was resting seemed to disappear. I was wrapped in this comforter as a child may be swaddled in a blanket of love by its father or mother. I felt the gentlest peace and love fill my being and was aware of being lifted up. The next morning I woke in the physical and felt well rested, refreshed, and happy with the memory of the amazing experience of being tucked in at bedtime as never before.

It seems remembering those moments when Soul was raised up in consciousness was more important than remembering the dreams that continued on through the night. The experience helped me grow in realization that I am Soul, a Divine spark of God. As Soul I can travel safely under the guidance of God's Prophet. I have learned that I am loved and given the experiences that are perfect for my spiritual unfoldment. God's timing is perfect.

Over time and with daily practice of singing HU, I have come to know that the spiritual beings who nourished me with comfort and love are Prophet and his co-workers. That experience showed me I am divinely guided and protected when traveling the vast inner worlds in the dream state. It is very reassuring to be in the presence of the one who knows the way, knows me, and knows my needs on my journey home to the Heart of God. Once you are touched by the Hand of God, it is not easily forgotten. The experience of God's Love is different from the experience of human love and cannot be measured or explained in words. The human standard of what I thought love to be has changed as my view of Divine Love grows through personal experiences with the Divine. With a sincere intent and prayer in your heart to experience Divine Love, it can happen. I am grateful for the outer and inner guidance available through Prophet, the Comforter of our time.

Written by Ann Atwell

51

Meeting an Inner Guide

Soul is programmed to return home and will eventually wake up to this yearning. When it does, the quest for a teacher begins. God always has a Prophet here on Earth to lead Soul on this journey home and to help us live an abundant life while here.

One night when I was in my late teens I came out of my room and told my Dad, "I feel like I'm waiting for my spiritual teacher." Dad did not have an answer to the statement and it puzzled me as well. Deep inside I was waiting for someone. I did not even understand for what or why, but something was missing in life.

I really appreciate that as my parents followed their hearts, they helped me follow mine. Dad had given me what I knew of God and religion. He brought me to Unity church as a young child and then to a Self-Realization Fellowship, but I could not commit to a teaching. When I was nineteen, my parents drove me from Michigan to the Catskills of New York to stay on an ashram for a month. After learning chants, doing yoga four hours a day, and eating a vegan diet, I left no closer to the spiritual peace I had not consciously felt in this lifetime, and yet I missed.

I was then given a beautiful dream. Although I did not know it at the time, it was an answer to my prayer for a spiritual guide. This dream meeting and the fact that I was allowed to recall it was a profound gift from God. I hold this as one of my most sacred treasures. I dreamed I was in a sea of golden light inside a giant golden bubble. There were smaller lights all around me like fireflies floating softly in the shimmering golden dome. A man came up to me with open arms and embraced me. I only saw him from his neck to his waist…he wore a long-sleeved blue garment.

I experienced in that moment a love deeper, fuller, and more amazing than words can describe. I felt more complete, deeply joyful, and a sense of truly coming home. When I awoke it was clear what I had experienced was real, and there existed a love unlike anything I had ever felt. This was proof to me there was more out there. There really was more to this life!

A few years after this dream my parents told me about the Nature Awareness School. They had been to a couple classes and had found something truly special. It was there I learned the man from my dream was real. At first I thought maybe he was my future husband. The love I felt in his embrace was as deep and vast as the ocean. I learned he is the inner and outer teacher, a Prophet of God. He could help me find the way to my true Heavenly Home again if I applied the necessary effort.

I was then allowed to become one of his students. My relationship with the Prophet has changed my life from the inside out. He has given me, among other spiritual treasures, the deep peace I somehow knew was missing but never felt until now.

Written by Carmen Spitale

52

A Spiritual Awakening

We can experience the Light of God in the waking state, or like in the following example, the dream state. Either way, our initial experiences with God's Light are often to "wake us up" from our slumber and inspire us to make the journey home to God. It is the Love of God that draws us home.

A little over ten years ago I attended my first class at the Nature Awareness School called "Wild Edible Plant Weekend." I did not know at the time how much this choice would transform my life in beautiful, abundant ways. All I knew was I was looking forward to spending a weekend in the mountains away from the everyday humdrum of city life. Upon arrival I felt something special about this place. Peace entered my heart and I enjoyed the beauty that surrounded me. On the surface this was just a wild edible plant class, but I felt something deeply spiritual stir within me that weekend.

After the class I had a vivid dream of flying down the gravel road that leads to the school. I saw Del, who I now know is a true Prophet of God, and his wife Lynne sitting on a bench outside their home. As I flew towards them they stood up and I saw beautiful white light shine around them. The light was stunning and would have been too much for human eyes, but through the eyes of Soul I found this light welcoming and nurturing. I said, "I don't know why I am here," and they replied, "Well, we are glad that you came." This was the Light of God shining through them to me, and the love, Divine love, I felt flowing from them awakened the true me, Soul, a Divine spark of God.

This dream was a gift of love from God through His Prophet to help me wake up spiritually. The spiritual tools Del has taught me for the past ten years have allowed me to accept my divinity as Soul and make God a reality in my life. This precious and sacred gift of knowing from experience that my Heavenly Father loves me and has sent His Prophet to show me my way home, is something I cannot keep to myself. My heart sings to be an instrument of God, to give and receive Divine love, so other Souls, like you perhaps, may awaken to your Divine nature as well and truly know God loves you and His Prophet is here to help show you your way home.

Written by Shanna Canine

53

The Other Side of the Glass

Only a thin veil separates the physical and spiritual realms. When this distinction is removed we can perceive the reality we actually live in: a world of Spirit.

In June of 2002 I attended my first class at the Nature Awareness School, a weeklong Personal Awareness Retreat in the Blue Ridge Mountains of Virginia. At one point during class a hummingbird flew into the open end of the school building and seemed to be having difficulty finding its way out the other side. Del walked over to where the bird was struggling and opened a window, allowing the little bird to pass freely through the opening. As he walked back to his chair he said something that struck me in a profoundly personal way, "It's okay to ask for help." A feeling of expansiveness came over me in that moment, as if a window had been opened for me also. Before then I lacked awareness that help from a Divine source was available.

That night the soothing sounds of nature could be heard as I lay down to sleep. My sleeping bag was comfortably nestled on a bed of straw within a cozy shelter near the pond. A good distance across from me laid a few other students who had already settled in for the night. As I closed my eyes I reached out to God, praying in a quiet whisper, "Please help me." I do not recall my request being any more specific. I just wanted God to know that if help really was available, I was open to receiving it. Later that night I was gradually awakened by the increasing discomfort of a full bladder. Reluctant to venture outside the shelter alone, this being my first real camping experience, I struggled to find a comfortable position that would allow me to put off a trip to the port-a-john until morning. I tossed and turned before surrendering to the inevitable conclusion that I was not going to make it that long. Sitting up, I noticed a faint light shining on the wall above one of the students who lay sleeping on the other side of the enclosure. Initially I rationalized that someone must have fallen asleep with their flashlight on, but something was different about the light I saw. Leaning forward as if I was peering around a corner for a closer look, I saw the softly illuminated sphere appeared to grow in size, forming an oval-shaped window of sorts with six discernable sides. To my amazement I was suddenly able see clear through the shelter to the woods that lay on the other side, where it appeared as though dawn had just begun to break.

A palpable stillness and energy permeated the night air. A young Native American man bearing a staff in his hand stepped quietly into the frame. Shortly after, the right shoulder of an elder came into view next to him. His skin appeared ancient, darkly tanned, and deeply lined with wrinkles. I sat motionless, watching in stunned amazement as he reached his hand slowly through the opening. As the hand moved toward me, I sensed it grow in size and take on a translucent, bluish-white glow before coming to rest over the fire pit that lay just beyond the foot of my sleeping bag. Its very presence seemed to beckon me from within to reach out and take hold.

Moments later the image was gone, and the lodge was once again pitch dark. I paused, slack-jawed, staring into the night, the image of the hand still fresh in my inner vision. The physical urge that initially woke me had likewise mysteriously vanished, leaving me free to savor the moment. As I laid back down and closed my eyes, I imagined what it might be like to crawl into that giant hand and rest there. The deep sleep I fell into afterwards brought with it an extremely vivid dream experience of swimming upstream against a strong current, determined to reach the top where I saw Del standing at the river's apex.

As I shared my experiences with the class the following morning, Del assured me that my experiences were real, as real as anything I might read about in the Bible. At that time he was quick to downplay his appearance in my dream, pointing out that Divine Spirit may take any number of forms one is comfortable with, as a gift of love to the dreamer. His efforts were always directed toward helping students develop an inner relationship with the Prophet of the times. My dream was indeed a prophetic one. On October 22, 2012, Del Hall III received the mantle of responsibility as the current Prophet.

It was the Hand of God that personally reached out to me during that first class back in 2002, and invited me to step into a whole new reality. Since then I have been taught methods for cultivating greater degrees of awareness and appreciation for the Presence of God that is with me and all Souls constantly, as the Prophet of the times. I have been shown my true identity as Soul, supported in facing my biggest fears, and given many tools to help me take steps toward manifesting my Divine nature and realize an ever more abundant life. Just like the little hummingbird I witnessed being escorted to freedom, by taking Prophet's hand, I have been redeemed in ever-greater degrees from the human state of consciousness. I have found love beyond my wildest imagination, peace in the most profound sense, and happiness in abundance on the other side of the "glass." Through a sincere prayer, followed by taking the Prophet's outstretched hand, all these gifts have been added unto me, and my life has been transformed in ever more beautiful ways.

Now, as in every age, a true Prophet of God is alive in our very midst to show us the way home to God. His hand appears in countless, tailor-made ways to personally bless, uplift, and guide us to our true home in the Heart of God. Perhaps my story will inspire you to reach out to God and ask His Prophet for help and guidance.

Written by Sandra Lane

54

The Golden Key

Prophet gently unlocks our hearts and minds to his presence and to the Love of God at a pace that is perfect for each of us. To receive too much, too fast, would be counterproductive. Prophet will often make his presence known with a blue light. This can happen in a dream or during the waking state. Either way, it is an invitation to accept the hand being offered and a reminder that we are never alone.

A few months after I attended my first spiritual retreat in 1998 at the Nature Awareness School I had a very special dream. At the retreat I learned my dreams were real experiences worth paying attention to, and I could learn, grow, and have spiritual adventures in my dreams as Soul.

In my dream I was walking in a meadow along a crystal clear stream that seemed to sparkle as it meandered through the green grass. The sunlight seemed to illuminate everywhere I walked. As I walked, I came to a bright blue flower next to the stream that became animated and seemed to want to show me something. The flower turned a bit, and it seemed to be pointing to a rock near the stream with its little leaves. It sort of nodded and said, "Hey, look over there." I looked at and around the rock but did not notice anything in particular. I had this feeling though there was something very special going on; I just had not recognized it yet. I looked back at the blue flower and it continued pointing to the rock. I then turned the rock over and hidden beneath it was a golden key. The key had golden light shining all around it. Reaching down, I picked up the glowing key and held it in front of me with both hands. Holding the key I felt light, free, and surrounded by a warm love. I took the key on my journey and woke up feeling very light and happy.

When I was given this dream I was excited. I did not know what it meant at the time, but I knew it was very special. I did not know much about Prophets or the Heavenly Worlds, but I had begun singing HU and had started to pay more attention to my dreams. Even though I did not recognize it at the time, this was a gift from God through His Prophet. God was reaching out to me in a way I could accept and understand without shocking my mind.

Early on, Prophet would let me be aware of his presence with a flash of blue light, or in this case a blue flower, and show me the way to something new. The blue light of the flower was showing me the way to a better life fulfilling the dreams of Soul. Over time, because of my spiritual teacher Del Hall I have been taught to recognize and become fluent in the language and nature of the Divine. This has been accomplished by the personal experiences that have blessed my life since becoming a student at the Nature Awareness School. These experiences have given me a whole new life which I feel very blessed to be living. The golden key I was given years ago has unlocked my heart to my true divinity, God's endless Love, and the Heavenly Worlds.

Written by Mark Snodgrass

55

My Personal Invitation

One of the very first things shared with new seekers is the importance of gratitude. It is something one's need for is never outgrown. The beauty of gratitude is that it opens your heart to the many blessings of God. One of the greatest being the Prophet, which God always has on Earth to help show His children the way home. Those with the eyes to see will recognize this eternal teacher within its current physical incarnation.

In 1996, as a result of a brochure we received, my wife and I decided to take a class at the Nature Awareness School. Neither one of us really knew where the brochure came from or how we got it, but it appeared at the perfect time and changed our lives forever. During one of my first classes I was offered the opportunity of a lifetime, though at the time I did not understand my good fortune. Since then, through an incredible spiritual journey and adventure, I have learned about my true self and have developed a more personal relationship with God.

God, through His Prophet Del Hall, opened my eyes to see more clearly what is truly real and valuable in life. He offered to show me the way back to my true home in the Heart of God. I did not understand what he was offering at that time, but deep inside I recognized something extraordinary in what I heard in Del's voice and saw in his eyes. One afternoon we did a spiritual exercise using a technique called wide-angle vision. During the exercise my spiritual eye seemed to open more fully. I knew I had been given a gift. I could now clearly perceive things with a new view and a deeper awareness. Everything looked, felt, and sounded different. I experienced a depth and richness in a way I had not before.

Later in the day my wife and I wanted to talk with Del. I remember noticing something unusual about this conversation. In the middle of the busy classroom everything appeared to move around us as if we were not in the same physical space as the other students present. It was as if we were in some kind of special, quiet, protected bubble. Near the end of the conversation Del mentioned that before we went to sleep we should think of some things we were grateful for in our lives. He said gratitude would open our hearts to Divine love, which we had just been talking about. Then he suggested we pay attention to our dreams and to fill him in the next morning.

Before I went to sleep I did as he suggested and thought of the things, people, and experiences I was grateful for in my life. Shortly after, in that in-between state where you are not fully awake and have not yet drifted off to sleep, I saw a bright orange and yellow light dance into my view. This light looked like a ball of fire or like the burning bush Moses saw referred to in the Bible. I had never experienced anything like this light before. The ball of spiritual light, looking like fire, changed into an intense white light, which slowly turned into what I could best describe as a blue tinted moon or ball of blue light. This ball of light rose up and out of a beautiful shimmering body of water and Del spiritually appeared before me. He gestured to join him, and we walked off together. In the morning before I could share anything about my experience from the night before, Del casually mentioned that in the dream state he had come and taken my wife and I to a spiritual temple to meet "his Boss." How could he have known what we had experienced last night? Both my wife and I remembered going somewhere with him in our dreams but nothing after going or any of the specifics.

It has taken many years for me to gain an understanding and to recognize the depth of the blessings offered during that early weekend retreat. I did not have the awareness or conditioning at that time to remember details of where Del took us on the inner planes. But over time with his loving guidance, more experiences, training, practice, and grace, I have been able to remember and benefit more and more from these travels into the inner worlds. Through these experiences and Del's guidance, I have learned how much God really loves us and that He always has one of His Prophets to guide us home to Him. I wish everyone could know how much God loves them.

Since that early class I have been escorted by Prophet to many of God's spiritual Temples of learning. As Soul, a child of God, I can be taken by God's chosen representative to learn more about who I truly am and why I am here. It is through the guidance of Prophet who shares experiences with God's Light and Sound, and especially God's Love, that we come to know and learn more about God. In hindsight, I realize on that night many years ago, through Del, God had personally extended His Hand and Love to me, and I accepted. My relationship with the Prophet of God has made it possible for me to truly accept God's Love and Grace.

Del is now offering others a similar opportunity to the one he offered me many years ago: a chance to consciously go home to Heaven, to visit God, and to experience the love He has for you. I am so very grateful I accepted!

Written by Jason Levinson

56

Dream Brings Treasure From Heaven

Dreams play a big part in our spiritual growth and provide us an opportunity to experience the Light and Love of God. At times our dreams also show us what the future may bring. They can plant the seed for the dreams of our heart to manifest here in the physical.

We were on vacation. I stretched out in the grass enjoying the warmth of the sun and the delicate breezes flowing across the water. I picked up my brush and added a few more strokes to the canvas. It had been so long since I last painted! I was attempting to capture the beauty of the sun's reflection as it danced across the quiet rippling of the lake.

My husband Mark was there, along with my aunt, her husband, and her son. Mark and I were staying in a cabin that sat right on the lake. We shared a picnic lunch together and visited all afternoon. It was a pleasure to be together in this place.

We decided it was time to say goodbye. I walked through the dim interior of the cabin to meet my aunt on the front porch. As I stepped out, light brighter than many suns shone down upon us. I saw her swallowed up in blazing gold and white. It was God's glorious Light! It was moving and sparkling. Then I saw nothing but just was. To my surprise we began to sing together in perfect harmony. I became absorbed in the sound and seemed to rise higher while also staying still. Our voices were rich and the sound was unlike anything I had heard before. It was pure freedom and joy.

As I woke up from this dream experience, I could still hear the beautiful echoes of that heavenly sound and feel the warmth of God's loving Light washing over me. Not only had I but also my aunt been touched by God's Light and Sound. My aunt and I shared a pure love, Soul to Soul, for each other and also for God. Bathing in His glorious Light we could not help but sing. The singing itself was a beautiful blessing. It was so freeing and natural to be able to express love like that.

A year or so after I had this dream my aunt and her family moved to Houghton Lake,

Michigan. We decided to plan a visit to go see them and we rented a cabin on the lake just as in the dream. It was then that Prophet helped me see the connection. My dream was manifesting in my outer life! I began to realize this trip was a significant part of my spiritual syllabus and also would bless my family. I thank you Prophet for allowing me this experience and for blessing those I love.

Written by Carmen Snodgrass

57

Firefighting and the Light of God

The Light of God is real and you can experience it for yourself. This is because God still reaches out to bless His children with His Light in our times, not just in the past. The Light of God has everything you need and ultimately it is an expression of God's Love for you.

Flames thirty feet high. Water shooting out of a three-inch hose at four hundred and fifty gallons per minute. Charging into a smoke-filled building. Firefighters live for that stuff.

Tonight was a quiet evening at the firehouse. We only had a few minor calls, like accompanying the EMS to a local residence for "difficulty breathing." A nice calm night – the kind firefighters know is better, even if we live for action.

I had recently joined up with the local volunteer department. I was still getting to know everybody, and still getting used to spending one night a week on the lumpy bunk room mattress. Earlier in the day I decided to try something new; I brought my dream notebook with me to the firehouse. I had written my dreams down for years, but this was the first time I brought my notebook to the firehouse. Something told me I had to. That night I had an incredible dream. Del, my spiritual teacher, was sitting with me and another student. We were at Del's school, sitting close and facing each other.

Del began teaching, and as he did a solid beam of pure yellow and white light showered down upon us. It was pure light, brighter and more real than anything in the physical world. It was almost tangible, like light you could feel and touch. It didn't just shine, it went into me and through me. It cleansed me from the inside out. It was brighter than the sun, but not hot; it brought peace, stability, and balance, but most of all the incredible feeling of God's Love. I awoke feeling reassured, balanced, and uplifted. But most of all, loved.

The Light of God is available to us today. It is not just something to read about. God is a living God, with living Prophets, and He still communicates and blesses with His Light. This dream came at a time when I was a bachelor living by myself. It showed that even though I was "alone," I was not really alone. God's Love and Light were with me, everywhere, through His Prophet.

This experience was also an example of the Bible verse, "Draw nigh unto God, and He will draw nigh unto you." James 4:8 KJV I had "drawn nigh," or closer to God, by bringing my notebook to the firehouse. This was a tangible step to put my spiritual path first. God responded a thousand times over by blessing me with an intense and beautiful experience with His Light. I knew I had a duty to share this experience with others.

We didn't do any firefighting that night. It was just a "quiet night" at the firehouse.

Written by David Hughes

58

Studying at a Temple of God's Wisdom

Our physical bodies need to sleep, but our true selves, Soul, do not. Soul can travel into the inner spiritual worlds to continue with the lessons it is currently gaining wisdom on. Those under the care of Prophet have the added benefit of being able to visit God's Temples of learning.

After attending a few retreats at the Nature Awareness School with Del Hall, the Prophet, he started coming to me in dreams. Over time I started to notice a trend to these nighttime adventures. In most of the dreams he was teaching and leading discussions with a group of Souls, some of whom I recognized as fellow students and friends at the school. As my interest in the spiritual teachings grew, Prophet responded by guiding me in the dream worlds to complement the outer teachings. There is a great benefit to having a teacher who can teach on both the inner and outer states because there are limitations to having a teacher only on the outer. Sometimes I wake from a dream with a brief image or knowingness that I spent some time with Prophet. Other times I recall vivid details of the teachings and consciously retain a valuable lesson upon awakening. Each experience is another step on this grand journey.

Prophet is qualified to teach us in both the dream and awakened states. In the physical we often gather for classes at the Nature Awareness School. In the dream state Prophet can safely lead us to the Heavenly Worlds and continue teaching. These dreams evolved to where he guided me to visit spiritual "college campuses" that are actually God's Temples of learning. I was very fortunate to be invited to these holy sanctuaries.

In one such dream I attended a class in a small house where Prophet was teaching me and several other students. The decor was not fancy, with white walls and wooden benches, so as not to detract from the primary purpose of my visit to this sacred place. The atmosphere was very welcoming and loving. His teaching continued for what seemed like several days, even though it all happened in one night of dreaming. One day we walked outside the house as a group onto a beautiful college-like campus that was more glorious than anything I have ever seen on Earth. Perfectly manicured lawns were interlaced with walking paths and lovely landscaped gardens. The building architecture was spectacular, and the structures seemed to glow with a soft golden light. Prophet led us to a large stone building that rose into the sky and reminded me of a grand clock tower. He invited us inside, where we gathered in a quiet room, and explained to us how his presence is able to nourish and sustain Souls with Divine love. God's Love is Soul's lifeline; without it Soul would not exist.

Despite having this dream several years ago I still vividly recall the images and feel the Prophet's presence and love from this experience being in one of God's Heavenly Temples. Souls are taken to these holy places by Prophet to study and learn God's ways and experience God's Love. While this dream was certainly a wonderful adventure, the real pearl is being in Prophet's presence and experiencing God's Love. Thank you Prophet for guiding me on this grand journey.

Written by Chris Hibshman

Summary

The Pearl of Dream Study

You exist because God loves you. One of the many ways God communicates to you is through dreams. These are gifts of love in the form of guidance and insight into all areas of your life. Career choices, family relationships, health issues, and more can be improved by learning how to invite, remember, and better understand your dreams. The wisdom contained within dreams has the power to set you free from some of the earthly challenges.

Dreams provide opportunities for healing, offer warnings, answer prayers, allow you to visit with loved ones who have passed, and shed light on what keeps you from experiencing more joy and love in your life. Dreams also help you work through karma, overcome fear of death, find your true purpose, and recognize your divinity as Soul – an eternal spiritual being. Ultimately dreams allow you to experience the Light and Love of God and to meet spiritually with God's Prophet who can show you the way home to God.

You are loved by God, and the "pearl" of dream study is coming to know this through direct personal experience. Thank you for reading this book.

Nature Awareness School

Del Hall and his wife Lynne established the Nature Awareness School in 1990. They continue to facilitate spiritual retreats at the school, located in the Blue Ridge Mountains near Love, Virginia. Del is a graduate of the United States Naval Academy and has a Master of Science Degree from the University of West Florida. He was a Navy Fighter Pilot and Jet Flight Instructor.

Although Del has a technical background his passion is in helping other Souls recognize their Divine nature and the ways of God. Del has facilitated hundreds of spiritual retreats. During these retreats the Voice of God has responded in magnificent and life-improving ways.

On July 7, 1999, after years of service and intense spiritual training in the ways of God, Del attained spiritual mastership. His position was upgraded on October 22, 2012 when God ordained him to be His Prophet.

Del has learned to follow Divine guidance to the benefit of all who are open to personal growth. He teaches them how to have their own experiences with the Divine while fully conscious.

Del then helps with the understanding and integrating of these experiences into daily life. Abundance follows.

Del's son joined the school as instructor after fifteen years of in-class training to develop and lead the introductory spiritual retreats. Del IV also lives on the school property in the beautiful Blue Ridge Mountains with his family. He is a professional artist who attended the School of the Museum of Fine Arts in Boston. Del is nationally exhibited with paintings in over seventy-five public and private collections. To see a sample of Del's work please visit lightandsoundofgod.com

Del IV facilitates the "Tools for Divine Guidance" and "Understanding Divine Guidance" retreats, which are the first two steps in the Nature Awareness School's five step "Keys to Spiritual Freedom Program."

Del IV also teaches people about the rich history of dream study and how to better recall their own dreams during the "Dream Study Workshops," which he hosts around the country.

Contact Information

Nature Awareness School
P.O. Box 219
Lyndhurst, Virginia 22952

natureawarenessschool@gmail.com
(540) 377-6068

Retreat descriptions and schedule are
available on our website.

NatureAwarenessSchool.com

Weekly Inspiration

Nature Awareness School's online publication "Weekly Inspiration" contains many stories that show the Hand of God working miracles in people's lives. Stories include help with careers, health concerns, relationships, healing, daily guidance, day and night dreams, spiritual travel into the Heavens, and so much more. To sign up for free email notifications of new posts please visit **WeeklyInspiration.com**

Facebook "Weekly Inspiration"

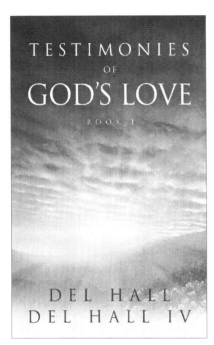

What if God is actively trying to communicate with you in order to bless all areas of your life but you do not know God's special language? God is a living God. He sends His Prophets to teach the "Language of the Divine" and to show His children the way home to their Father. Divine Love and guidance has always been and is still available to you. Learning how to listen, trust, and respond to this guidance will improve your life and bring more abundance to your heart.

Within these pages are miraculous modern-day testimonies written by students of the Nature Awareness School. Here they learned how to recognize God's guiding Hand in all areas of their lives. Through dreams, Divine insight, experiencing the Light and Sound of God directly, or traveling with an inner guide into the HEAVENS, these true stories show us God is indeed alive and still communicating. These testimonies show how God is reaching out and desires to develop a more personal and loving relationship with each of us.

These testimonies will shatter any perceived limitations to what is truly possible in your relationship with God and God's Prophet. They show how others are experiencing God's Love and Grace and will serve as inspiration on your own journey home to the Heart of God.

Visit Loved Ones In Heaven

Have you ever lost a loved one and longed for just one more moment together? What if it were truly possible to have this time together? Could a visit, if even for a brief moment of time, help heal your heart? Would knowing for certain that they still exist and are doing well bring you a deep peace? What if you could express your love once again? Imagine how that would feel!

Visiting loved ones in Heaven is possible! God can bless Souls separated by physical death by reuniting them spiritually for short visits. The authors of the testimonies in this book do not have to imagine what such a wonderful opportunity would be like. They each have experienced the profound blessings of such moments. They chose to share their experiences to praise the loving God that blessed them and to inspire you, the reader, to strengthen your own relationship with God. Within this book are spiritual tools and daily practices that may help YOU to have your OWN similar experiences.

These testimonies will shatter perceived limitations as to what is possible in your relationship with God and God's Prophet. Spiritually meeting departed parents, grandparents, aunts, uncles, children, close friends, and even beloved pets can heal broken hearts. These moments together also bless your loved one as they too desire to reach out to you. These beautiful and heartwarming stories are possible because God loves both you and your loved ones.

Testimonies of God's Love – Book Two

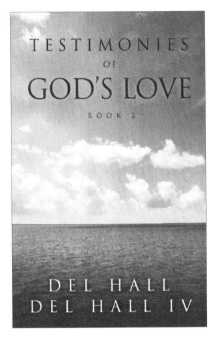

What if God is actively trying to communicate that He LOVES YOU, wants a personal relationship with YOU, and wants to bless all areas of YOUR life?

God's Love and guidance shine through every day in thousands of ways for those who know His language. He sends His Prophets to teach the "Language of the Divine" and to show His children the way home to their Father. Learning how to really see, listen, trust, and respond to this love and guidance will improve your life and bring more abundance to your heart.

Within these pages are miraculous modern-day testimonies written by students of the Nature Awareness School. It is here they learned how to recognize God's Love and guiding Hand in their lives. Whether through dreams, Divine insight, experiencing the Light and Sound of God directly, or traveling with an inner guide into the HEAVENS, these real experiences show that God truly loves us. These testimonies illustrate how God is reaching out and desires to develop a more personal and loving relationship with each of us.

These testimonies will shatter any perceived limitations as to what is truly possible in your relationship with God and God's Prophet. They reveal how others are experiencing God's Love and Grace and will serve as inspiration on your own journey home to the Heart of God.

Prophet Shares God's Light

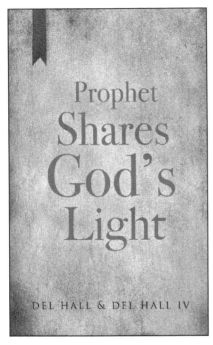

What if God's Light and Love rained down on you like something out of scripture? It happens to ordinary everyday people, not just famous spiritual legends from the past.

God is a living God. He continues to use His Light as a major way to deliver blessings to His children. These blessings include love, peace, joy, wisdom, truth, clarity, healing, and so much more. The testimonies within this book share how experiencing God's Light can bring wonderful and profound abundance into your life.

These true stories are written by students of the Prophet of our times. He personally helped them grow spiritually and prepared them to experience God's Light. The Prophet then aids his students in understanding the blessings that are encompassed in the Light by teaching the "Language of the Divine."

After years of being conditioned in His Light, some of these blessed Souls have even returned home spiritually, while still living, to the Abode of God. They were shown the way by the Prophet, who is authorized to share God's Light and lead His children home.

If you hunger to have a FULLER and more LOVING relationship with God, more than what most could ever imagine, this book is for YOU. Please read it with a heart full of gratitude – thankful for the courage of those who contributed to this book, wanting only to bless YOU as they have been blessed.

Testimonies of God's Love – Book Three

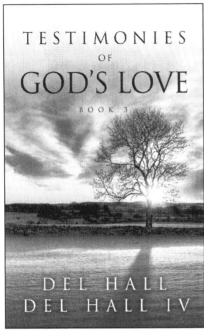

God expresses His Love to YOU every day in many different and sometimes subtle ways. Often His Love goes unrecognized because the ways in which God communicates are not well known. Learning to recognize and accept God's Love and guidance brings abundance into your life.

The testimonies in this book show many different ways God reaches out to His children. These true stories will expand your understanding of God's language, the "Language of the Divine." Profound and heartwarming testimonies of God's Love and guidance are being shared by students from the Nature Awareness School. It is here that God's Prophet, Del Hall III, takes his students from being seekers of God to finders of God and of their true eternal selves, Soul.

This book will expand your understanding of what is truly possible in your own relationship with God and God's Prophet. You will also learn how having a living Prophet who is ordained by God as your teacher can greatly assist your spiritual growth.

If you hunger to have a MORE ABUNDANT and more LOVING RELATIONSHIP WITH GOD, more than what most could ever imagine is even possible, this book is for YOU.

Love is Demonstrated – Making Marriage Sacred Again

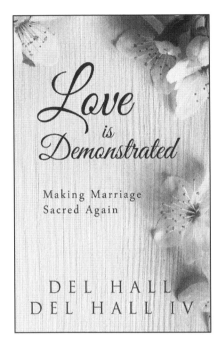

Marriage is not simply a day of celebration but a lifetime of demonstration.

"Happily ever after" is a fairy tale because it suggests that once you find love, you are all set. Just fall in love, get married, and enjoy a lifetime of happiness together. The truth is, merely loving your spouse is not enough. Your love for one another must be demonstrated, in ways you can both accept, for it to be of actual value.

Within these pages are eight stories from four marriages that were transformed by a closer relationship with God and His Prophet, Del Hall III. The stories show how when you seek first the Kingdom of Heaven all other things can be added unto you. This includes a fulfilling and loving marriage.

No two marriages are the same, yet one can learn and be inspired by these stories. The insights and wisdom contained in this book have the power to improve your relationship or marriage, even if it is already good.

Made in the USA
Charleston, SC
16 October 2016